The Roman Colosseum

Other titles in the *History's Great Structures* series include:

History's Great
STRUCTURES

The Roman Colosseum

Adam Woog

ReferencePoint
Press®

San Diego, CA

For Stu Witmer, a scholar and a gentleman.

© 2014 ReferencePoint Press, Inc.
Printed in the United States

For more information, contact:
ReferencePoint Press, Inc.
PO Box 27779
San Diego, CA 92198
www. ReferencePointPress.com

LIBRARY OF CONGRESS CATALOGING-IN-PUBLICATION DATA

Woog, Adam, 1953-
  The Roman Colosseum / by Adam Woog.
    pages cm. -- (History's great structures series)
  Includes bibliographical references and index.
  ISBN-13: 978-1-60152-540-6 (hardback)
  ISBN-10: 1-60152-540-0 (hardback)
  1. Colosseum (Rome, Italy)--Juvenile literature. 2. Amphitheaters--Rome--Juvenile literature.
  3. Rome (Italy)--Buildings, structures, etc.--Juvenile literature. I. Title.
  DG68.1.W66 2013
  945.6'32--dc23
                                                                    2013001182

CONTENTS

IMPORTANT EVENTS IN THE HISTORY OF THE ROMAN COLOSSEUM

326 BC
The Circus Maximus, a huge amphitheater for chariot races and athletic contests that was a predecessor to the Colosseum, is built.

177
Emperor Marcus Aurelius passes legislation in an attempt to stop violent gladiator games.

80
Vespasian's son Domitian formally opens the stadium with one hundred days of games and exhibitions.

217
The stadium is severely damaged by fire.

50   100   150   200

96
The death of Domitian signals the Colosseum's slow descent into disuse.

CIRCA 70
Vespasian begins construction of the Colosseum.

313
Emperor Constantine I's conversion to Christianity hastens the end of gladiator games.

AD 69
Vespasian becomes emperor and establishes the Flavian dynasty.

404
Gladiator games are banned.

2012
Archaeologists find traces of paintings on the Colosseum's inside passageways during the restoration project.

1920s
Dictator Benito Mussolini orders archaeological work that exposes the Colosseum's hypogeum.

1805
Napoleon I of France begins archaeological work on the Colosseum while occupying Rome.

523
Staged animal fights and hunts are banned.

500   **1000**   **1500**   **2000**

1349
The most serious of the earthquakes to damage the Colosseum occurs, and the structure continues to decay and suffer neglect.

2011
The largest restoration and renovation project in the Colosseum's history begins, cleaning and strengthening it and making much of it accessible to the public for the first time in centuries.

1749
Pope Benedict XIV declares the Colosseum a sacred Christian site.

INTRODUCTION

In the Days of the Gladiators

The air in the huge stadium is hot and motionless, the late afternoon sun still burning. The crowd in the bleachers, roaring at top volume, can smell the sweat and blood of the gladiators as they fight to the death in the arena below. The screams of animals as they were slaughtered in the morning still seem to echo around the stadium as do the cries of condemned criminals who were brutally executed later in the day. The scene of these images is the Roman Colosseum, two thousand years ago.

As the millions of people who visit it each year know well, the Colosseum is a priceless relic of the ancient Roman Empire—the most famous surviving building from the days of that once-glorious realm. Many centuries have passed since the stadium rang with the sounds of gladiatorial games, and its appearance today provides only a glimpse of its former splendor. Its discolored walls, once a brilliant white, have crumbled or, in places, completely fallen. Its elaborate statues, paintings, carvings, and other decorations are long gone. The seats from which emperors, statesmen, and ordinary Romans once cheered and booed are cracked and empty. And the arena itself is now a huge open hole—a gaping, mysterious warren of underground tunnels and chambers.

And yet, despite its diminished condition the Roman Colosseum still has the power to fascinate nearly two thousand years after it was dedicated in AD 80. This is true not only because it is visually stunning—even as a ruin—but for other reasons as well. For one, it is simply an astonishing feat of architecture and engineering, the largest freestanding stadium ever built at the time it was completed. Some of the ways in which it was constructed and how it worked are mysteries still to be unraveled. Perhaps most of all, the Colosseum has always been a vital symbol of the mighty Roman Empire, which for centuries controlled a huge portion of Europe, the Middle East, and North Africa—the largest empire the world had ever known.

Today, the Colosseum's imposing size and mysterious, romantic allure have made it the most famous landmark in Rome—an icon as easily recognizable and as beloved as the Eiffel Tower in Paris or the Statue of Liberty in New York City.

> **WORDS IN CONTEXT**
> icon
> *A treasured symbol.*

Moving Past Nero

The Colosseum was built during boom times, in the first century AD when the Roman Empire was beginning to peak in expanse and power. The stadium's construction began under the auspices of one emperor, Vespasian, and was finished by two more: his sons Titus and Domitian. Together, these three were the Flavian Dynasty, and this title gives the Colosseum its original name: the Flavian Amphitheater. It has been called "the Colosseum" only since the eighth century.

For Vespasian, building his gigantic stadium was a sharp political move. He had many rivals who wanted to take his place, so he needed the approval and backing of Rome's leaders, aristocratic class, and ordinary citizens. He also knew that a sure way to appeal to these people was to supply them with food and entertainment—"bread and circuses," as the phrase went. Building a structure where people could attend lavish amusements—for free—was a perfect way to deliver at least some of this bounty.

The choice that Vespasian made for the future stadium's location was also politically shrewd. He had become emperor soon after the death of a ruler widely despised for his cruelty and selfishness: the infamous Nero. By demolishing Nero's lavish palace in the heart of

The Colosseum (pictured) was built at the peak of the Roman Empire's size and power. Rome's grand amphitheater, which offered free and spectacular entertainment to all citizens, was built by the emperor Vespasian to win the support of his subjects.

Rome and building a new public stadium in its place, Vespasian took a major step forward in cementing his popularity.

Unspeakable Cruelty

The kinds of entertainments that Vespasian and his successors offered the public were not new. Gladiator fights—mock battles between trained warriors—had existed in Roman culture for centuries. Other elements of a typical day's program were also familiar, notably the execution of criminals and the display (and often slaughter) of exotic animals.

The difference was that the Colosseum was far larger than any previous stadium ever built—capable of seating an estimated fifty thousand people—so the shows had to be correspondingly grand. The stadium's opening ceremonies set the tone for these gargantuan spectacles: one hundred days during which thousands of animals, convicted criminals, and gladiators would be killed.

These games seem unspeakably cruel today. It is difficult to imagine that society could accept, for entertainment purposes, the mass slaughter of animals, brutal public executions, or gory battles during which gladiators fought to the death. These violent acts might be acceptable to some people in the context of a movie or video game—but not in real life.

Modern society may judge them harshly, but by the standards of ancient Rome such performances were not extreme. Gladiator games were indeed bloody, but this brutality reflected some of the most fundamental ideals of Roman life: nobility, strength, loyalty, virtue, and honor. The contrast between the ancient Romans' tolerance for brutality and their respect for strength and honor is striking. Writer Judith Testa points out, "[It] simultaneously calls to mind the greatest and the most repulsive qualities of ancient Roman society."[1]

In some ways the ancient Romans' appetite for violence is still very much alive. Humans were attracted to violence and fascinated with death long before the Colosseum was built, and this might still be true long after today's sports stadiums and video games are gone. All the ancient Romans did was use this attraction and fascination to produce entertainment on a gigantic scale. The result: the Colosseum—the structure that proclaimed to the known world that the Roman Empire was the mightiest anyone had ever seen.

CHAPTER ONE

The Roman Empire

For centuries the Roman Empire was the most literate, sophisticated, and militarily powerful culture in the world. From the imperial city of Rome a succession of emperors reigned over a vast territory. At its peak in the first and second century AD, the empire covered some 2.2 million square miles (5.7 million sq. km) and took in much of Europe, North Africa, and the Middle East.

The Romans sent armies and administrators to every corner of this sprawling realm. Organized and powerful, the Romans maintained the territory already under their control while relentlessly expanding into new lands. They built bustling cities and infrastructure such as roads, bridges, and water systems to support them. This work has proved so durable that many examples of it—including the Colosseum and its many imitations—still survive, in some cases more than two thousand years after they were built.

Rome also extended its highly developed culture across the empire. Latin, the language of the Romans, became the standard tongue and formed the basis for today's Romance languages: French, Spanish, Italian, Romanian, and Portuguese. Roman customs, religious beliefs, arts, and government structure also became standard—although some local customs remained in many regions. Estimates of the immense Roman Empire's overall population vary widely, from 65 million to 130 million, representing somewhere between 20 and 40 percent of the world's inhabitants.

This empire was a huge, solidly built, and smoothly running operation. Its frontiers were secure, and law and order were generally maintained. Its infrastructure was efficient and innovative. There were certainly negative aspects to the empire, including the practice of slavery and frequent instances of religious persecution. But in general the *pax Romana*—the Roman peace—worked well.

Nero

But the peace and order of the Roman Empire did not last forever. The realm collapsed in the middle of the fifth century, in part because of devastating invasions along its borders by barbarian tribes.

Before that, however, when the empire was still strong, its ruling class prospered, largely because of the immense wealth that poured in from the provinces in the form of taxes and other revenue. As this class grew wealthy, it also grew complacent and dissolute. Although most people within the empire's borders led at best modest lives, Rome's royal and upper classes could enjoy pampered lives of leisure, self-indulgence, and materialistic excess.

In particular, the excesses of Emperor Nero, who reigned from AD 54 to 68, dramatically symbolized the ruling class's overall air of decadence. Nero loved to organize huge orgies of feasting and sex, and he loved theater and games such as festivals featuring chariot races and athletic and musical contests.

Nero, who considered himself a talented singer, musician, and actor, often performed in public himself. This was scandalous behavior, because the ancient Romans considered actors and performers to be shady and perhaps even immoral. Allegedly, Nero forbade any spectator to leave the auditorium while he was performing. A historian of the time, Suetonius, claimed that a woman gave birth during one of the emperor's recitals, and that men pretended to die so that they would be carried out of the theater.

Perhaps the most blatant example of Nero's self-centered extravagance was a huge, ornate palace he had constructed for himself, the Domus Aurea ("Golden House"). It featured three hundred rooms,

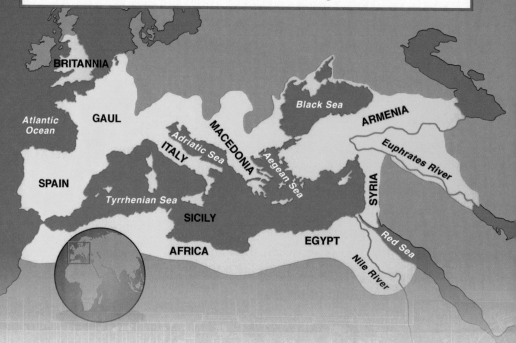

marble walls, numerous fountains and pools, and a revolving ceiling powered by slaves. During banquets, ivory panels in the hall's ceilings rotated to shower rose petals on the guests, while a system of pipes sprinkled them with perfume.

Nero also had a reputation for extreme cruelty and was directly or indirectly responsible for many deaths. When he was young his mother, Agrippina, arranged for the murder of his half-brother so that Nero could become emperor. Later, Nero had his mother murdered because she stood in the way of his desire to divorce and remarry. According to legend, he also persecuted early Christians—who were then a minor religious sect—by torturing them or burning them at night as a source of light for his palace.

The Great Fire

During Nero's reign a massive blaze in the heart of Rome in the year 64 created an opportune location for what would later become the

Colosseum. Known as the Great Fire, it began in a neighborhood of shops selling flammable goods and spread quickly. It burned for about five days and destroyed three or four of Rome's districts (accounts vary) and severely damaged seven others.

Nero is widely believed to have deliberately set this fire in order to clear land for his Golden House. This belief gave rise to the familiar phrase that the emperor "fiddled while Rome burned." (If true, the instrument would have actually been a stringed instrument called a lyre, since fiddles did not exist in ancient Rome.) But many historians have questioned this belief that Nero was responsible for the arson.

They point to a number of factors that make it unlikely. For one thing, fires were very common in ancient Rome; major blazes occurred in 69 and 80. Also, Nero apparently was sincere in his efforts to ease the city's suffering in the aftermath of the blaze. He had been away from Rome at the time, on the southern coast of Italy, but rushed back to the capital when notified of the blaze. According to several reliable sources, he personally took part in the search for and rescue of victims. The emperor may have also opened his palaces to provide shelter and food for people whose houses were destroyed.

Furthermore, after the fire Nero enacted new building codes such as creating wider and straighter streets to give firefighters better access, ordering that platforms be built on wooden structures so that fires could be more easily fought, and arranging for better ways to access water throughout the city. And he was eager to rebuild damaged portions of the city through measures such as paying bonuses to Romans who rapidly rebuilt their houses. Finally, skeptics ask, why would Nero have needed to set the fire in the first place? The powerful emperor could have simply taken any piece of land he desired.

Despite these few noble acts, Nero was unarguably a cruel dictator. For example, he tried to blame the fire on members of a new religion—Christianity. According to some sources, he rounded up Christians and ordered that they be torn apart by dogs or crucified. He may even have burned some of them alive to provide lighting for

his homes at night. And others he simply executed in public. These "shows" were popular among many Roman citizens, and in a sense they may have laid the foundation for the bloody gladiatorial games that would become so popular with the public.

A New Emperor

Finally in 68 the despised emperor met his downfall. A revolt in the northern territories, which was mainly a rebellion against Nero's unfair taxes of the countryside, spread and ignited riots and similar widespread uprisings across the empire. The senate, the chief body of Rome's lawmakers, declared that the increasingly erratic Nero was no longer fit to rule. Leaders within Rome's military refused to fulfill his orders. The senators of Rome further declared that he was a public enemy, meaning that anyone could kill him without punishment, at which point the powerful Roman military moved to take over. Nero's staff and bodyguards deserted, and the emperor was forced to flee the city. Faced with almost certain execution, he committed suicide.

A struggle for leadership immediately ensued, resulting in growing turmoil and chaos. In the space of a single year after Nero left his throne, four men crowned themselves emperors in turn, but only the last was able to sustain his rule. This was Vespasian, who managed to hold onto power for ten years, from 69 to 79. Vespasian was a capable leader who led a simple life and condemned Nero's excesses and corruption. The new emperor restored order to his increasingly chaotic realm, reestablished discipline in the army, made the government more responsive to ordinary citizens, and put the empire's finances on an even keel.

Vespasian carried out his plans with a keen sense of how to gain and keep power—by winning the favor of both the aristocratic class and ordinary citizens. He knew that people who were content with their lives would be less likely to turn against him. And one dramatic way to do this would be to build a magnificent amphitheater in the imperial city—the biggest stadium the world had ever seen. This structure was to be a venue for entertainment and diversions, free to all Roman citizens and appealing to all of Rome's strictly divided social classes. In this way it became a symbol of how amusements can keep people happy and perhaps divert their attention from other matters. The Roman poet Juvenal called this giving the people "bread and circuses."[2]

There were other reasons for undertaking the project as well. For one thing, Vespasian wanted to distribute more equitably the riches (in taxes and other forms of revenue) that were pouring in from lands that were being newly added to the Roman Empire. Constructing his stadium would serve this purpose to a degree, by giving the ordinary people of Rome some of the benefits of this bounty. Archaeologists Keith Hopkins and Mary Beard comment, "In building the Colosseum Vespasian was dramatically making the point that the profits of Roman military success belonged, in part at least, to the common people of Rome; it was not only emperor and aristocracy who were to enrich themselves with the booty of empire."[3] In addition, a massive construction project like the Colosseum would help solve unemployment problems among commoners by creating thousands of jobs.

And there was another, broader motivation behind Vespasian's plan. The emperor envisioned the Colosseum serving as a model for stadiums in smaller towns elsewhere. He knew that these imposing structures would be striking symbols. They would be constant visual reminders to people all across the empire—people who had once been independent—of Rome's dominance. Writer Nigel Spivey notes, "From north Africa to south Wales, essentially similar structures were raised."[4] And by the end of the second century, well over two hundred of these versions of the Colosseum had been built.

Choosing a Location

Vespasian shrewdly selected as the site for his new stadium a place with deep symbolism: the grounds of Nero's Golden House. Vespa-

BREAD AND CIRCUSES

The phrase "bread and circuses" was coined to describe what Roman emperors often felt was all that was needed to keep their people happy and entertained. In this passage the Roman historian Dio Chrysostom describes how the Roman population reacted when provided with the pleasures of a spectacular "circus," even in the days before the Colosseum's lavish shows:

> [They are] a people to whom one need only throw bread and give a spectacle of horses since they have no interest in anything else. When they enter a theatre or stadium they lose all consciousness of their former state and are not ashamed to say or do anything that occurs to them . . . constantly leaping and raving and beating one another and using abominable language and often reviling even the gods themselves and flinging their clothing at the charioteers and sometimes even departing naked from the show.

James Grout, "Circus Maximus," *Encyclopaedia Romana*. http://penelope.uchicago.edu.

sian knew that demolishing this symbol of the former dictator and reclaiming the land for public use would strengthen his campaign to cast himself as a benevolent leader. The Roman populace would thus better appreciate the differences between Vespasian and the still despised Nero. Historian Chris Scarre comments, "The whole affair was a massive public relations exercise."[5]

Nero's extensive grounds included, in addition to the palace itself, several other buildings, extensive gardens and woods, and an artificial lake fed by a canal diverted from a nearby stream. The fact that the Golden House was in the center of Rome was an added benefit. Typically, outdoor theaters throughout the Roman Empire were built on the outskirts of a city, but the Golden House lay in the heart of the empire's greatest urban center. One modern commentator notes,

"Vespasian's decision to build the Colosseum on the site of Nero's lake can also be seen as a populist gesture of returning to the people an area of the city which Nero had appropriated for his own use. In contrast to many other amphitheatres . . . the Colosseum was constructed in the city centre; in effect, placing it both literally and symbolically at the heart of Rome."[6]

The cost of construction is unknown, although an inscription found on the site provides a clue about how it was financed. It states

Competitions get under way at the Colosseum, as depicted by an early artist. Vespasian spent lavishly on the project in an effort to portray his rule as benefiting the common people and not just the aristocracy.

that funding for the project came from the riches that poured in from Rome's military conquests. The bulk of these riches likely came from Rome's recent success in stopping a rebellion by the Jews in Roman-controlled Palestine. One of the outcomes of the empire's victory in this conflict was that its armies returned to Rome laden with valuables from the treasury of the main Jewish temple and other sources. The Jews were also forced to pay extra taxes, which further increased Rome's profits. Norma Goldman, an American archaeologist who has extensively studied the Colosseum, comments, "No one will ever know how much in cash was poured into the project, but it was money well spent, since it assured the popularity of the ruling family, and the royal treasury had [no] bottom."[7]

The Gladiatorial Tradition

The concept of a stadium for contests and games had its origins in the distant past. The Colosseum was by no means the first of its kind in the Roman Empire, or even the first one in Rome. Small amphitheaters for athletic contests and other entertainment could be found all across the realm. In Rome the largest and best known of the stadiums was the huge Circus Maximus, which dated from 326 BC.

Although the Circus Maximus was generally used for chariot races, it was also home to other forms of entertainment. Notable among these were fights between gladiators—that is, combatants who fought mock conflicts based on genuine warfare.

The origins of gladiator games (*munera* in Latin) are uncertain, but they probably originated as funeral rituals for members of the aristocracy. There is evidence that

WORDS IN CONTEXT
propitiated
Appeased, soothed, made calm.

prisoners or slaves were forced to fight each other during these rituals. Tertullian, a writer of the first and second centuries AD, states, "[M]en believed that the souls of the dead were propitiated by human blood, and so at funerals they sacrificed prisoners of war or slaves of poor quality bought for the purpose."[8]

TYPES OF GLADIATORS

By the time the Colosseum was built, the rules of gladiator games were well established. So were the main fighting styles and the types of weapons and armor that were used. Sometimes gladiators who fought in the same style were matched with each other, but more often warriors with contrasting styles were pitted against each other. Among the main types of gladiators:

The *secutor* used a large shield and a helmet that covered the entire face.

The *retiarius* was armed with a trident (three-pronged spear) and a net, and was protected by only a small shield worn on the left shoulder.

The *murmillo* was armed with a long spear and wore a helmet with a fish-like crest.

The *thraex* carried a curved sword and a small, square shield.

The *sagittarius* was an archer on horseback.

The *hoplomachus* fought with a small, round shield; carried a lance and short, straight sword; and often wore leather armor on his arms and legs.

The *essedarius* fought from a chariot.

The *cestus* fought with his fists, using only a crude form of boxing glove.

The *eques* fought on horseback.

The *laquearius* used a noose or lasso to bring down an opponent.

The *velites* threw javelins and sometimes wore headdresses made of wolf skins.

The *dimachaerus* used a sword in each hand.

The *andabata* wore a helmet with no eyeholes and so fought blind.

Among the surviving evidence of this practice are third-century BC tomb paintings that depict teams of fighters, armed with helmets and weapons, taking part in an elaborate burial ceremony. But the practice may be much older; evidence shows that similar traditions were part of Greek culture stretching back to at least the eighth century BC.

The contests held at funerals had strong religious overtones, being rites of sacrifice held to present offerings of blood to the gods. Historian Fik Meijer writes, "They believed that the blood of prisoners gave the dead strength for the difficult journey to the underworld."[9] Over time, these rituals became increasingly elaborate. For example, in 65 BC Julius Caesar commemorated his father, who had died twenty years earlier, with a performance by 320 pairs of gladiators in silver armor.

Gradually, ceremonies honoring the dead came to include not only gladiatorial contests but other kinds of spectacles. One such ceremony was a grandiose memorial service Caesar sponsored for his daughter Julia, who had died eight years earlier. These performances, held at her tomb, included stage plays and fights between wild beasts as well as displays of exotic African animals, including the first appearance in Rome of a giraffe. Even in the days before the Colosseum was built, these entertainments were extravagant and expensive—the costs of importing animals from Africa were especially heavy.

Over the course of a few centuries, the ceremonies lost their religious significance. They were increasingly used by politicians, who handed out tickets in order to curry favor, or by wealthy Romans who wanted to show off their ability to afford lavish amusements. What had once been solemn funeral rites became little more than after-dinner entertainment. Nicolas of Damascus, a historian who lived in the first century BC, notes, "When everyone had had plenty to eat and drink, they called for the gladiators. The moment anyone's throat was cut, they clapped their hands with pleasure."[10]

From Sacred Rite to Popular Entertainment

As the spectacles grew in popularity, variety, and sophistication, they became more complex. For example, it was no longer enough to simply stage a battle between warriors. It became increasingly commonplace to mount elaborate exhibitions demonstrating the differences between Roman styles of fighting and those of peoples from outside the empire.

Performances involving exotic animals were also part of this increased trend toward showiness. Suetonius, writing about one such event in the previous century, states, "Fights with wild animals were held for five days in a row and the whole show concluded with 500 foot soldiers, twenty elephants, and thirty horsemen on each side. To make more space for the battle the turning posts [of the chariot race course] were removed and in their place two camps were set up facing each other."[11]

As the popularity of the games grew, strict customs developed around them. Gladiators were overwhelmingly men, although records indicate that a handful were women. Most were convicted criminals or prisoners of war. The Roman army's remarkable success in conquering new lands provided a constant supply of these captured prisoners. Many of these prisoners were forced into slave labor in the empire's mines or at other manual labor, but the most robust among them were trained as gladiators.

Some gladiators, however, were not convicts or prisoners of war but former soldiers who were accustomed to violence and found that being professional gladiators helped relieve the difficulty of adjusting to civilian life. And some were ordinary Roman citizens who volunteered as a way to escape their lower-class or impoverished circumstances. For them, becoming a gladiator was a better option than a life of poverty. The schools where gladiators trained offered regular meals, housing, and a measure of security—and volunteers also stood to gain riches and a measure of fame if they prevailed in the arena.

Even at the height of the gladiator era, when the Colosseum was the mightiest stadium in the world, the warriors who fought there were almost universally considered low class and held in contempt by Rome's aristocracy. Meijer notes, "To the patricians the gladiator was a rough, frightening outsider, a doomed man beyond hope of reprieve, an utterly disreputable slave."[12]

Yet there were exceptions. A gladiator who fought bravely was admired for his courage. The Roman philosopher and statesman Cicero asserts, "Down-and-outs or barbarians they may be, but just like well-brought-up men, they'd rather take a hit than dodge in cowardly fashion."[13] This was certainly true as far as the ordinary citizens of Rome were concerned. They generally did not hold gladiators in such contempt or regard them as inferiors in class. Instead, they typically celebrated the exploits of their favorite warriors and followed them closely, much as modern-day sports fans follow their favorite athletes.

This admiration for a gladiator's courage reflected a fundamental aspect of Roman culture, and it also indicated the deep symbolic importance the games had in that culture. Seen in one way, Roman gladiator fights were little more than violent entertainments. But they also represented the Roman ideals of the glory of warfare, military-style discipline and loyalty, and dying a noble death. Gladiators who faced their opponents bravely and battled well were certain of glory even in death, and the best of them were lucky enough to survive as superstars. This was a powerful inspiration for the ordinary Roman, notes James Grout in the *Encyclopaedia Romana*: "The gladiator demonstrated the power to overcome death and instilled in those who witnessed it the Roman virtues of courage and discipline."[14]

The gladiatorial games' shift over time from sacred rite to popular entertainment was criticized in some quarters. For example,

Tertullian complained that such performances flattered the living—they did not honor the dead. And other commentators deplored the increasing amounts of flashiness and violence they saw. But such criticisms were rare. Gladiatorial games were in general immensely popular, and that popularity reached its peak in the first century AD, just as Vespasian ordered construction of his spectacular stadium to begin.

CHAPTER TWO

Design and Construction

By today's standard, building the Colosseum was not a swift procedure. However, by the standards of the era, and considering the project's huge scope, it went quickly. It was essentially finished within a decade. The precise year of the start of its construction is uncertain—most reliable sources estimate the date to be between 70 and 72. The stadium's grand opening was in 80, so the construction phase was eight to ten years.

The building's architects and builders are unknown. At the time, architects and builders were usually considered craftsmen and hired hands rather than highly skilled artists. Judith Testa comments, "In imperial Rome it was the patron who counted; the architect often was merely an anonymous employee."[15]

Despite their lowly status, however, the stadium's creators were clearly talented. The design they made was practical, well proportioned, and pleasing to the eye. The plans called for an oval-shaped stadium with a total length of 660 Roman feet and a width of 540 Roman feet. (A Roman foot, called a *pes*, varied slightly according to region, but it was generally around 11.5 inches [29.6 cm]). The interior of the stadium had three basic parts: the *cavea* (seating area or bleachers); the podium (the imperial terrace, where the emperor and his party sat); and the central arena in which the games took place.

Around the stadium's outer wall the architects designed a set of eighty graceful arches (curved shapes that support walls or other heavy loads) that would serve as entrances and exits. Inside, between the outer wall and an interior wall, ran a complex series of elaborately decorated walkways, ramps, and stairways. These allowed spectators to come and go in an orderly way. They were called *vomitoria*, after the Latin word for "expel," because they allowed the crowds to exit quickly.

Techniques and Tools

Little is known about how the Colosseum's architects and craftsmen went about their work. Nonetheless, archaeologists have been able to piece together a rough picture of how the stadium was designed and built. This limited knowledge is mostly based on what is known about ancient Roman building techniques in general. Many of the Colosseum's design features can be seen in the construction of older structures, so it is likely that the Colosseum's architects used methods, techniques, and tools that were well established by the time their work began.

For example, architects had long used tools such as floor plans drawn to scale, three-dimensional scale models, and full-size design sketches—tools still used by modern-day architects. Using these techniques gave the architects the ability to convey their plans to the Colosseum's artisans and construction overseers—that is, the skilled workers responsible for turning their designs into a reality.

The stadium's specific design elements would also have been familiar from earlier buildings. For example, the Colosseum made frequent use of arches and vaults (passageways with arched ceilings). Roman builders of bridges, buildings, and other structures had long understood the aesthetic and engineering advantages of these construction methods. Arches, for example, enabled builders to construct long, sturdy bridge spans, walls, and roofs. The Romans did not invent such techniques, but they did perfect their use.

Another design element that also borrowed from well-established traditions involved the use of rows of columns similar to those used in other Roman buildings and, before them, ancient Greek structures. The Greeks had developed three major styles of column: Ionic, Corinthian, and Doric. These styles differed mainly in their decorative touches, but all were frequently used for structural purposes—to hold up roofs. The Colosseum's columns, by contrast, did not bear any weight. They were placed on the outside of the outer walls and were purely decorative.

Along with these trustworthy tools and design elements, the stadium's builders used building materials that were similarly tried and true. Notably, concrete was a primary building element for the Colosseum. The Romans had long used in their buildings an early form of concrete, which was a mixture of water, lime, ash, and pumice stone. Typically, once this concrete was set it was then overlaid with a layer of bricks, which provided a much more pleasing look.

Building the Foundation

Once the details of the Colosseum's basic design and construction were established, the work could begin. Vespasian and his sons had access to an essentially limitless workforce for this. Some of the workers were skilled artisans or other free men who were paid for their efforts. But slaves performed the bulk of the manual labor, both in the stone quarries where the raw material was dug and on the construction site. Estimates of the number of these slaves vary widely, from twenty thousand to one hundred thousand. Likely, most of them were prisoners of war, especially Jews, from regions of the Middle East that the Romans had recently conquered.

The first task for these workers was to demolish what remained of Nero's Golden House. Then they created a system of drains in the area where the Colosseum was to be built. These drains diverted the stream that had fed Nero's artificial lake and so dried out the land to a degree.

The next step was to create the Colosseum's foundation. This involved, among other arduous tasks, digging deep into the ground with pick and shovel. Since the land was still somewhat marshy, and

A close-up view of the Colosseum's interior shows the honeycomb of stairs, ramps, arches, and passageways that made up the structure. Little is known about the architects and craftsmen who designed and built the Colosseum.

since the weight of the Colosseum's walls and arena would be enormous, workers had to dig until they reached a solid floor of clay.

The laborers next poured concrete mixed with rocks for the foundation. Some of this concrete was likely recycled from the rubble of Nero's palace. The foundation was laid at a different thickness in different places. Under what would become the arena, for instance, the foundation was about 13 feet (3.96 m) deep. Under the stadium's walls, meanwhile, the foundation needed to be roughly 42 feet (12.8 m) deep—the walls would need much more support than the arena. The exact depth varied slightly from area to area, depending on the clay floor beneath the foundation.

The foundation for the walls was further strengthened with brick retaining walls along both the inner and outer edges. This massive foundation, laid down in many layers, spread the weight of the walls and bleachers across a large area and thus made them less likely to fall. This foundation, roughly 39.3 feet (12 m) deep, later served to raise the floor of the Colosseum higher than ground level. Meanwhile, the dirt that had been dug out to make room for the foundation was used to also raise the ground surrounding the structure (that is, outside the walls) about 21 feet (6.4 m). The result raised the overall level of the building so that it was higher than the buildings around it and all the more imposing.

Building the Walls

Once the foundation was in place, the work of building the stadium's walls could begin. This involved building both the inner and outer walls as well as the honeycomb of stairs, ramps, and passages in between that would be used by spectators to reach their seats.

Among the primary building materials for these sections were huge blocks of stone from quarries near the town of Tivoli, which is some 18.6 miles (30 km) from Rome. At the quarry, workers excavated and cut the stone into rough blocks, which may have then been finished on the construction site to ensure a close fit. However, it is also possible that most of the shaping work was completed at the quarries. Norma Goldman comments, "There is evidence of skilled work done in stone yards for pieces brought already cut and finished to be installed, as is done today in modern construction projects."[16]

The stone used for the load-bearing walls consisted primarily of two forms of limestone: tufa and travertine. Bricks were used for decorative stone facades on the outside wall; brick, tufa, and marble were used for decorating the interior as well.

The project required staggering amounts of material: an estimated 240,000 horse-drawn cartloads of travertine were quarried for the Colosseum's exterior walls alone. This translates to an estimated 106,000 cubic yards (100,000 cubic m) of stone. It has been estimated that the entire building required about 750,000 tons (688,388 metric tons) of common stone, 8,000 tons (7,257 metric tons) of marble, and 6,000 tons (5,543 metric tons) of concrete.

The individual blocks of travertine were enormous, measuring as tall as 20 feet (6.1 m). These huge blocks were brought to Rome on barges along the Tiber River, which cuts through the city. They then traveled by oxcart to the building site, about 1.5 miles (2.4 km) away from the wharves where they were off-loaded.

It has been estimated that during the construction period a cart carrying a load of travertine left the Tiber wharves on average every seven minutes for twelve hours a day, three hundred days a year. This activity undoubtedly created a massive disruption to daily life—the ancient Roman equivalent of heavy traffic. Chris Scarre comments, "Carts carrying materials for public building works were among the very few allowed in the city during the day, and the steady stream of heavily laden vehicles through some of the busiest parts of Rome must have been a constant concern to the inhabitants, as well as a constant reminder of the project at hand."[17]

As the walls rose, the stone blocks used for the higher levels were lifted and set in place by human-powered cranes. No mortar was used to attach the stones to each other. Instead, large metal clamps held them in place. The clamps themselves weighed about 300 tons (272 metric tons) in all.

Finishing Touches

With the basic structural elements in place, the Colosseum's builders could focus on some of the finishing touches. For example, on the ground level, the arena—where the action took place—had a wooden floor with a layer of sand on top. (The Latin word for sand, *harena*, is where the English word *arena* comes from.) The arena's surface was designed to be roughly 13.1 feet (4 m) below the first row of seats, ensuring that everyone in the audience would have a clear sight line to the activity. This also lessened the risk of a wild animal jumping out of the arena into the spectators. Nonetheless, the stadium's designers knew that this was still a possible danger. So they added an extra layer of safety for the emperor and his party: A kind of huge net, made of rope and elephant tusks strung on a wooden framework, was wheeled in front of the imperial viewing box during events.

Another final touch involved decorating the stadium's three stone stories. The walls of the Colosseum featured a number of decorative

 THE CIRCUS MAXIMUS

The Colosseum was by no means the only stadium in the Roman Empire—not even the only one in the city of Rome. The largest and best known of the city's stadiums was the huge Circus Maximus, built in 326 BC with an estimated capacity of 150,000 spectators. This structure no longer exists, but evidence suggests that it was a long, oval-shaped racecourse where chariot races and athletic contests were held. When it was built, the Circus Maximus was unpretentious: little more than rows cut into a hillside for seating that overlooked an open field. Over time it was renovated with features that were later reflected in the Colosseum's structure, including a ceremonial entryway for contestants, seating made of stone, private boxes for dignitaries, and an imperial box for the emperor and his retinue.

touches in addition to their built-in vaults and arches. One example was the outer wall's decorative columns, with a different design on each level. Since these were only decorative, they were half-columns, with the flat sides flush to the wall. Also, the arches above the ground story held huge, beautiful bronze shields and statues of emperors and mythological figures. And nestled in an archway above each entrance was a gilded horse-drawn chariot.

In addition, the Colosseum's walls were painted brightly or decorated with carvings. Many of these touches no longer exist, having decayed or been pirated away over the centuries, but a few have survived. Examples include partial carvings on the interior walls of the stadium, showing a variety of animals, people, and scenes. Scholars Peter Connolly and Hazel Dodge comment about these: "Two fragments show dogs hunting deer; others have animals such as dolphins, griffins and sphinxes in static positions."[18]

The Hypogeum

While most of the Colosseum was finished before Vespasian's death in 79, it was left to his sons to complete the work. The elder of these sons, Titus, ruled from 79 to 81. His brother Domitian succeeded him, reigning from 81 to 96. Titus finished construction enough for the grand opening in 80, but Domitian was responsible for the bulk of the additions that came later. For example, he added the fourth floor, the wooden story used mostly for storage, and he completed the seating areas. But his main contribution was the addition of the hypogeum, an intricate underground complex beneath the arena. (*Hypogeum* means "below ground.")

The Colosseum's hypogeum was designed and built about two years after the stadium opened to the public. It remains unclear today why the hypogeum was added later rather than being constructed when the stadium was first built. A two-story warren of interconnected, tightly packed chambers, stairs, ramps, and tunnels, the hypogeum held participants, animals, and props until they were needed for performances in the arena above. Existing stadiums elsewhere already used similar underground facilities, but these earlier versions were smaller and simpler than those of the Colosseum. The ingenious designers of the hypogeum created a highly organized and efficient "shop" in which many complex tasks could be carried out at the same time. Animals, performers, and stagehands with props gained access to the hypogeum through tunnels leading in from outside the stadium, and once inside, they were housed in one of the facility's many rooms.

When something or someone was needed in the arena, workers used a system of elevators, some of which were specially strengthened cages for transporting wild animals. The elevators worked using a simple method. A rope attached to the top of an elevator passed up and over a pulley set into the ceiling. The rope and pulley were connected by gears to large, horizontal wheels turned by four men on each of the hypogeum's two levels. As the men turning the wheels created enough power to pull the rope, the elevator rose. Then they could let the elevator down in reverse, by slowly releasing the rope. Vertical channels cut into the walls of the underground chambers guided the elevators smoothly up and down. Some of these channels are still visible, as is a series of semicircular cuts in the walls, which were likely carved out to make space for the revolving wheels that the men powered.

WORDS IN CONTEXT
pulley
A wheel over which a rope can pass to lift heavy weights.

Exactly how many elevators there were is unclear, but research suggests that the hypogeum housed three large cages and several smaller ones. Also unclear is how very large animals, such as giraffes or elephants, were brought in. They would not have fit in the tunnels leading to the hypogeum, much less in the elevators that led from there to the surface.

The hypogeum's arrangement seems crude by today's standards, but in many ways it was a remarkably efficient and well-organized system, representative of the planners' attention to detail. This high degree of organization was especially important considering the underground facility's limited space. Heinz-Jürgen Beste, a German archaeologist and an expert on the hypogeum, comments that the facility had "countless ropes, pulleys and other wood and metal mechanisms housed in very limited space, all requiring endless training and [discipline] to run smoothly during a show. Like a ship, too, everything could be disassembled and stored neatly away when it was not being used."[19]

The Awning

As with the hypogeum, the designers and builders of the Colosseum created another ingenious apparatus for the day-to-day operation of the stadium. This was a huge awning or canopy that could cover a large section of the bleachers. Its primary role was to shade audiences, protecting them from the fierce Italian sun. Goldman comments, "This was a pampered audience, and in the entire Mediterranean, people did not want to sit out in the hot sun."[20] The canopy was used only for shade. It could not be used on windy or rainy days—it would not have withstood rough weather.

Like the hypogeum and many other features of the Colosseum, the awning, called a velarium, was not a new invention. Earlier stadiums elsewhere in Rome and around the empire had used similar equipment. Not surprisingly, however, the one developed for the Colosseum was far larger than any others, in keeping with the stadium's oversized nature.

The velarium was retractable—that is, it could be furled or unfurled like a ship's sails as the need arose. It was probably made of linen or cotton, although some architectural historians have suggested that the material was silk. Silk was (and is) very expensive, but Rome's emperors rarely spared expenses where their stadiums were concerned. For instance, Nero appears to have had an awning made of silk for his stadium. Woven through it was an image of the emperor driving a chariot. Whether silk, cotton, or linen, the Colosseum's awning required a huge

The Layout of the Colosseum

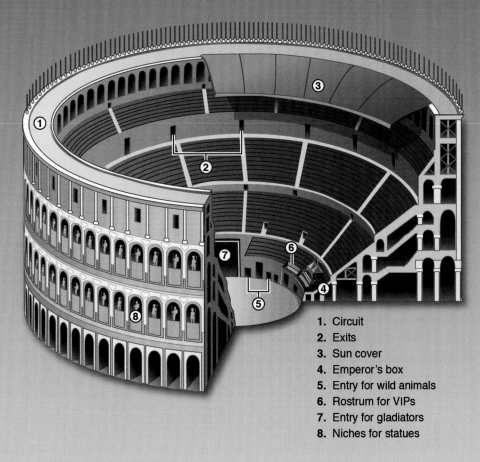

1. Circuit
2. Exits
3. Sun cover
4. Emperor's box
5. Entry for wild animals
6. Rostrum for VIPs
7. Entry for gladiators
8. Niches for statues

Source: University of Massachusetts, "Landscape Architecture Study Tour: Roman Colosseum," 2010. www.courses.umass.edu.

amount of cloth. Assuming it was made of linen, the weight of the cloth alone has been estimated at about 24 tons (21.7 metric tons).

The velarium may have been colorfully dyed, although this has not been definitively proved. According to surviving documents from a poet of the time, the awnings of Nero's amphitheater had been dyed purple, red, and yellow. As sunlight shone through them, the spectators appeared to be bathed in those same colors. But the Colosseum's canopy required such vast amounts of cloth that it may have been impractical to dye it similarly.

The method of operating the canopy is unclear and has been the source of controversy among scholars. The cloth was likely unfurled from the fourth story of the stadium on long, horizontal wooden poles that pointed inward toward the center of the stadium. These would have been similar to the arrangements on the vertical masts and horizontal booms of a modern sailing ship, which allow sails to be easily furled and unfurled. When it came time to bring the velarium in or out, workers used a complex arrangement of ropes and winches to pull the "sails" along the booms.

The velarium's poles were probably made from pine and fir trees, two varieties of trees that grow tall and straight and that also could be found easily in the countryside around Rome. They were likely stored on the stadium's fourth floor when not in use and extended from there, slotted securely into holes in the walls when in operation.

The velarium probably covered only about two-thirds of the stadium bleachers. The arena itself remained uncovered. At certain times of the day dignitaries seated close to the action would not be protected. However, they likely brought their own umbrellas or canopies with them.

A permanent team of sailors, estimated at about one thousand, was kept on hand to operate the huge canopy. It was undoubtedly a great honor for a sailor to be chosen to live in Rome and work at the famous Colosseum. Only the most skilled sailors would have been chosen—that is, those who understood well the actions of ropes, sails, and wind, since sudden changes in wind direction or speed could lead to disaster.

Bollards

Some archaeologists have suggested that a different system might have been used to operate the awning. Perhaps, they propose, it rest-

OUTSIDE THE COLOSSEUM

The Colosseum was not the only building that the architects of the stadium planned when they designed the structure. The area immediately surrounding the stadium was also home to several large outbuildings that serviced the main structure. One of these was the *armamentarium*, a storage facility for weapons and armor used in gladiatorial games. Large props and equipment were housed in the *summum choragium*. And in the *sanitarium*, wounded gladiators received medical care. In addition, the Colosseum grounds included four gladiatorial schools to teach specific styles of fighting. For instance, the *ludus matutinus* was a facility that specifically trained men for combat against animals.

ed on a system of ropes that extended over the stadium in a kind of giant spider's web, kept in place by ropes anchored outside the stadium walls. But this is regarded by many archaeologists as unlikely, in large part because of the difficulty of anchoring the ropes securely.

According to this theory, the system would have used stones called bollards that were set in the ground outside the stadium. Originally, 160 bollards ringed the outside of the facility about 57 feet (17.4 m) from its exterior walls. Archaeologists know that the bollards existed, although only one of them still remains.

The problem with the bollard theory is that the bollards were not set securely in the ground. They would not have supported the great weight of the awning—instead, they would simply have been ripped out of the ground. A more likely explanation for the existence of the bollards is that they were barriers that aided crowd control. When an event was about to begin, chains would have linked the bollards to each other in a circle around the stadium, keeping eager crowds from getting in too early. Probably the chains were then moved so that they resembled the spokes in a wheel, allowing orderly lines to form as spectators entered and, after the performance, exited.

The completion of the Colosseum in time for a grand opening in 80 reflected the careful planning and arduous labor that had gone into the building's construction. The ingenuity of the Colosseum's designers and builders helped fulfill the stadium's most important purpose: to delight those who attended its lavish performances—especially by satisfying the Roman taste for violent entertainment.

CHAPTER THREE

The Spectacles

The Colosseum's grand opening celebration in the year 80, overseen by Titus, set the tone for the future of the stadium. Over the course of 100 days, tens of thousands of men and animals were slaughtered—5,000 on one day alone, according to one account. Subsequent games maintained this convention. For example, the emperor Trajan celebrated a military victory in 107 with games that reportedly resulted in the deaths of 11,000 animals and 10,000 gladiators over the course of 123 days.

These figures are undoubtedly inflated, if only because the logistics involved in bringing such huge numbers of animals from Africa would have been beyond the capabilities of even the ingenious Romans. Nonetheless, the Colosseum's spectacles were undeniably at the extreme edge of violence. One reliable document recounts the details of a festival held in 240: 2,000 gladiators killed, along with 70 lions, 40 wild horses, 30 elephants, 30 leopards, 20 wild donkeys, 19 giraffes, 10 elk, 10 hyenas, 10 tigers, 1 hippopotamus, and 1 rhinoceros.

Announcing an Event

When a game was organized, its sponsors advertised the event with hired criers or graffiti written on walls around the city. Advertisements provided details about the upcoming *munus iustum atque legitimum* ("proper and legitimate gladiator show"). They mentioned the game's date, the number of gladiators scheduled to appear, and other attractions.

No announcements specifically for Colosseum events are known to have survived. However, archaeologists discovered an ad for a performance at the stadium in the city of Pompeii. According to this announcement—preserved, as the entire city was, by volcanic lava in 79—the show included performances by musicians dressed as animals, including a flute-playing "bear" and a horn-blowing "chicken."

The games at the Colosseum, advertised in similar ways, were the talk of Rome. Virtually the entire city was eager to see whatever show was on offer. An anonymous writer of the time comments, "Before the games, who talks of anything else, either in the home or in the tavern?"[21]

Admittance to a performance was, in theory, free for all Roman citizens. However, there were some restrictions. Notably, although the stadium was huge, its capacity was limited, so tickets were highly prized. Evidence suggests that some were given out to curry political or economic favors, much like sought-after tickets to sporting events today. Keith Hopkins and Mary Beard write, "Our guess is that, even though the shows were free, the poor and the very poor were systematically under-represented. . . . If this is correct, the audience at the Colosseum was more of an elite of white toga–clad citizens than the rabble proletariat [working class] often imagined today."[22]

Bringing the Crowd In

On the day of an event, the lucky ticketholders lined up outside the stadium in front of one of its arched entrances. The general populace used seventy-six of the stadium's eighty entrances. The others were reserved for special attendees and dignitaries. The emperor and his party had their own private entrance, which led under the seats to the imperial box close to the arena.

To move spectators in smoothly and quickly, the Colosseum had a highly organized system of crowd control. Tickets, which were usually made from pottery, bone, or wood, informed spectators which of the stadium's entrances to use. By climbing a series of ramps and stairs, then matching their tickets with numbers carved in the stadium's walls, ticketholders could easily find their assigned sections and seats.

The manner in which the stadium's stairs and ramps were decorated reflected the social standing of the ticketholder. The lower walkways—the ones leading to the more desirable seats—were luxurious, with marble floors and walls and ceilings made of painted stucco. Higher up, where the less desirable seats were, the stairs and tunnels were narrower and less grand.

The seats were probably rather uncomfortable. They were made of stone, so many people brought cushions with them. Worse, they were cramped, averaging only about 15.6 inches (40 cm) wide and with about 27.6 inches (70 cm) of legroom—less than a typical modern-day economy class airline seat. Although Romans were generally shorter than Europeans today—the average adult male was 5 feet 5 inches (1.67 m) tall—such a small space would have allowed little room to move.

In the sections reserved for the higher classes, the strictly observed rules were based on social standing. Senators and other government officials sat nearest the emperor, or at least in the next tiers up. The names of some senators, carved into the stonework to reserve their seats, can still be seen in this section. A program's *editor* was also honored with a seat close to the emperor, although often the emperor and the editor were one and the same. Also occupying a place of honor were the vestal virgins, women of high social and religious status.

The next level up was reserved for lesser members of the aristocracy, and above them sat the general public. Generally, women were allowed to sit only in the very highest tiers, standing or sitting on wooden seats rather than the more prestigious stone or marble used for lower seats. And people with very low status, including gravediggers and actors, were banned altogether. With some exceptions, even retired gladiators were forbidden to attend a performance—they were

The bloody spectacles held in the Colosseum led to thousands of deaths—both of gladiators and animals brought in to entertain the crowds. On at least one occasion, an ancient document notes, the dead included thirty elephants along with numerous leopards, giraffes, and more.

considered too low-class to be worthy of a place to sit with even the humblest citizen.

The Games Begin

Normally, a program began early in the morning and lasted until late in the afternoon. As a typical day's audience moved into the stadium, the mood was already getting raucous. Fik Meijer writes, "The atmosphere in the Colosseum is quite terrifying, even at dawn. As thousands of spectators make their way to their seats, they can hear the trumpeting of elephants, the howling and barking of dogs and wolves, and the roars of lions and tigers coming from the cages beneath the arena."[23]

Once the crowd more or less settled in, the event formally began. First up was an elaborate procession of the gladiators and animals who would be appearing later in the day, accompanied by a small orchestra of musicians playing brass horns and drums.

Typically, the day's first individual event was a series of performances featuring unusual animals. By the time the Colosseum was built, the Roman appetite for exotic creatures had grown large, requiring constant infusions of new and unusual sights. The expanding empire's new colonies, especially in North Africa and the Middle East, were able to provide an almost constant supply, although at great expense. It became a point of pride for a show's editor to be able to present some astonishing new member of the animal kingdom to the public.

After the opening procession, these animals were taken back down into the hypogeum. When the time came for them to reappear, they were lifted from the hypogeum in their elevators, led up a ramp to the surface, and released. If necessary, the animals were encouraged to enter the arena by men who waved bunches of burning straw or wielded red-hot iron bars behind them.

Sometimes animals were not harmed during a performance, particularly if they were especially rare and prized. Such creatures were merely paraded around, and some were trained to perform tricks. For example, one observer of the time mentions an elephant that could write words in the sand with its trunk.

However, animal performances were not often bloodless. Frequently the creatures were pitted against each other in battle or against trained hunters armed with long spears in a performance called a *venatio*. Although they had been nursed back to health after their arduous journeys to Rome, animals destined for these battles had been starved before entering the stadium. This lent a degree of supposed realism to the proceedings, making the animals seem as fierce and eager to fight as possible.

WORDS IN CONTEXT
editor
In ancient Rome, the person, sometimes the emperor, who organized or produced a gladiatorial event.

In other attempts to add realism to these staged hunts, crews of painters, technicians, and carpenters had already adorned the arena with artificial forests, complete with real trees and bushes planted in the floor. Added excitement during a hunt was created by secret trap-doors in the floor, which opened to launch animals unexpectedly from the hypogeum below. Eyewitness accounts describe how animals appeared as if by magic during a performance to catch hunters off guard. Heinz-Jürgen Beste comments, "The hypogeum allowed the organizers of the games to create surprises and build suspense. A hunter in the arena wouldn't know where the next lion would appear, or whether two or three lions might emerge instead of just one."[24]

Death in the Arena

Another type of performance that re-created scenes from nature was the *silva*. Some of these shows were simply glimpses of natural environments provided for the entertainment of urban Romans. But they were often used as settings for dramatic performances, typically enacting scenes from mythology, and in that case they were usually, predictably, violent.

Many of the Romans' mythological stories recounted a legendary hero's death. Such a story reenacted in the Colosseum typically featured a condemned criminal as this hero—a part that inevitably ended with the actor's death. Writer Tom Mueller comments, "The Roman poet Martial . . . describes a criminal dressed as Orpheus playing a lyre [harp] amid wild animals; a bear ripped him apart. Another suffered the fate of Hercules, who burned to death before becoming a god."[25]

Another popular myth that was acted out in the Colosseum's arena was the one about the flight of Icarus. According to tradition, Icarus was able to fly using wings he had constructed, but fell to earth when the sun melted the wax in the wings. As enacted for the audience, this story became a performance that Nigel Spivey calls "a bungee jump without the bungee."[26]

After these performances, the midday portion of a day's program was typically the execution of condemned criminals and prisoners of war. These unfortunates were sometimes tied to stakes with signs identifying their crimes. After a period of time, fierce animals might be let loose to slaughter these *damnati*, as they were called. At other

THE ACTIVITY BELOW THE ARENA

While the audience in the Colosseum focused on the bloody events in the arena, the hypogeum below it was a scene of furious activity. Laborers performed their backbreaking jobs in humid summer and chilly, damp winter. The chambers reeked from years of accumulated smells of human sweat and wild animals. It was also dark, lit only by smoky oil lanterns. And it was deafeningly loud, with an overwhelming din of creaking machinery, people shouting, animals growling, and loud signals made by horns or drums to coordinate the complex series of tasks being carried out.

Then, when it was all over, there was an eerie calm—but the work was not finished. Historian Fik Meijer writes,

After the spectators have left the Colosseum, a powerful atmosphere of death and decay lingers in the underground passageways. Carcasses of wild animals lie everywhere, along with the corpses of executed criminals, horribly mutilated by the claws and teeth of predators. Everything is drenched in blood and there remains a penetrating odour of rotting flesh. But since there may well be another show within a few days, perhaps even the next day, everything has to look clean again. For the large permanent staff of the Colosseum and the extra manpower hired for the occasion, a dispiriting task now begins: clearing out all the corpses and carcasses.

Fik Meijer, *Gladiators: History's Most Deadly Sport*. New York: Thomas Dunne, 2003, p. 184.

times, the condemned men might simply be forced to fight one another. The last one standing might or might not be set free, depending on the whim of the emperor.

For a few years the Colosseum may also have seen reenactments of famous sea battles, using scaled-down warships. For these performances the arena would have been flooded to a depth of 3 to 5 feet (1 to 1.5 m). However, this use of the arena has been the subject of considerable debate among historians.

Skeptics point to a number of logistical problems. For example, they ask, how could the arena have been waterproofed? How, exactly, was water pumped into and drained from the stadium? And would there have been enough space for even small-scale warships to maneuver? None of these questions has been definitively answered. It has been suggested instead that reports of the Colosseum's mock sea battles may have referred to a lake (artificial or natural) in another location.

In any case, if reenactments of sea battles did take place in the Colosseum, they could have been mounted only during its first two years. Domitian added the hypogeum at that point, after which flooding the stadium would have been impossible.

Diversions

In between the major events were other performances, usually comic events or lighthearted games designed to amuse the audience. For instance, writers of the time noted performances in which boys rode on bulls, elephants danced, and mock gladiator fights were staged between farm animals wearing armor.

On one occasion, Emperor Gallienus, who ruled in the third century, punished a merchant who had tried to cheat the empress by selling artificial jewels to her. Gallienus forced the terrified merchant to appear in the arena, telling him that he would be pitted against a lion. But when an animal cage was lifted to the floor of the arena, only a chicken emerged. The crowd roared with laughter, after which the emperor announced that the merchant had been deceived, just as he had tried to deceive the empress. The humiliated jeweler was then allowed to return home.

Also between the main events, spectators could take part in gambling, which was a constant and tolerated activity. They could also try to catch wooden balls that Colosseum personnel hurled into the bleachers; these balls could be redeemed later for food, money, or other gifts. Not surprisingly, scuffling for these tokens led to still more entertainment: frequent fights that broke out in the audience.

Spectators could buy refreshments, such as cakes, pastries, dates, or wine, from roving vendors. Some people took formal lunchtime breaks, eating in nearby taverns, but others stayed all day. They could not afford a meal, did not want to miss a moment of the action, or were simply afraid that they might lose their seats.

The Main Events

All of these performances and diversions were simply warm-ups to the main events: the gladiatorial games. In a sense, the games had begun the night before, when the gladiators had been the guests of honor at a banquet. Open to the public, the banquet gave people the opportunity to see individual gladiators close up and assess their chances before gambling on them. For many warriors, of course, the banquet amounted to a last meal.

The games proper usually were held in the early afternoon and started when the warriors trooped into the packed arena from one of the stadium's reserved entrances. They marched in two by two, carrying their helmets and shields, as trumpets

WORDS IN CONTEXT

pompa
A formal parade of gladiators and other performers around the arena, held at the beginning of a day of performance.

blared, drums pounded, and the crowd roared. Following this procession, which was called the *pompa*, the gladiators saluted the emperor, standing in front of his box.

It is commonly believed that the gladiators uttered a ritual sentence, or some variation of it, at this moment: *"Ave, Imperator, morituri te salutant*" ("Hail, emperor, those who are about to die salute you"). However, many scholars believe that the phrase was used only once, at a mock naval battle on a lake in the year 52. There is no mention of another occurrence elsewhere in recorded history.

Training

Many of the gladiators who were about to appear were reluctant participants—prisoners of war or others who had to be forced to fight. However, some were members of professional troupes who traveled from city to city. In some cases, entrepreneurs managed these troupes, organizing shows and paying members' salaries.

Professional or not, the gladiators had typically trained in schools where they lived in military-style barracks while they received lessons, usually from retired gladiators. During these practice sessions, students learned the importance of discipline and self-control—necessary traits if a gladiator wanted to prevail in the arena. Peter Connolly and Hazel Dodge note, "Highly developed fighting skills and great control gave the gladiator the greatest chance of remaining alive in the arena."[27]

Gladiator schools typically trained students to excel in specific types of battle. Each of the many different kinds of specialized styles had its own equipment and moves. For example, some gladiators fought with swords and wore helmets that exposed only their eyes. Others wore helmets with no eyeholes at all, leading to contests that amounted to a deadly game of blind man's bluff. And some wore almost nothing and were armed only with giant nets and tridents (three-pronged spears).

Students were given blunt wooden versions of weapons to train with, to prevent fatalities, and they were generally treated quite well. Schools routinely provided massages, high-quality medical care, and nourishing meals. Since future warriors were considered valuable property, this was simply good business practice. Hopkins and Beard comment, "A dead gladiator was an expensive gladiator. Likewise mangy specimens were probably not crowd-pullers."[28]

⬡ THE VESTAL VIRGINS

The vestal virgins were always among the most honored guests at the Colosseum's games. They had their own special entrance into the stadium and their own box from which to view the performances.

The vestals were priestesses of high honor and religious significance, somewhat like nuns in today's world. They were responsible for several sacred tasks in the Roman religion, notably tending the sacred fire of the hearth, which symbolized the home and family. They also prepared sacred grain for sacrificial rituals and served as models of moral behavior.

There were eighteen vestals at a time: six young novices in training, six active vestals, and six retired vestals who were teachers for the novices. They lived in lavish quarters near the Colosseum. The vestals took vows of chastity—that is, they were obliged to remain virgins—during their thirty years of service. Afterward they could marry, although few of them did. The punishment for breaking a vow of chastity could mean being buried alive.

The Battles

Typically, battles began at a signal from the editor. The action was nonstop, and when the ground became soggy with blood it was covered with a fresh layer of sand. Captured warriors who were reluctant to take part in the fight were encouraged to change their minds through the use of whips, fire, and other punishments. This public torture was considered nothing more than another aspect of the day's entertainment.

Referees and their assistants oversaw most games. The referees had the power to stop a battle or call a time-out, giving warriors a chance to rest, get refreshments, and have their wounds treated. Referees also had the authority—which could be overridden by the emperor—to stop a fight if the gladiators were too exhausted to continue and there was no clear winner.

Generally, gladiators or groups of gladiators with similar skill levels were matched, although there were variations. For example, sometimes gladiators were deliberately matched in unequal teams. And condemned men were often required to fight in series: The game would start with one armed and one unarmed fighter. As might be expected, the unarmed man died. Then a third warrior attacked the armed fighter, the survivor of that battle fought another, and so on until only one remained.

The final performance of the day saw two top gladiators facing each other. Typically, they were especially skilled in contrasting styles. For instance, one warrior might be heavily armored and carry a sword, while the other would be almost nude and armed only with a net and trident.

If a gladiator wanted to quit and concede defeat, the usual signal was to throw away or lower his weapon and raise his left index finger. The emperor then decided the fighter's fate as the crowd shouted its opinions. A decision usually depended on how bravely the gladiator had fought. He might be spared, or he might be forced to kneel while his opponent delivered a deadly blow. A warrior who had fought bravely was accorded a merciful and noble death—a sword thrust downward through the neck. Others were not so lucky: They were crucified, burned, or torn apart by animals.

As the emperor pondered his decision, the crowd, worked up to a fever pitch, shouted phrases like *"Mitte!"* (Let him go!), or *"Lugula!"* (Kill him!). They might also display the thumbs-up or thumbs-down signal. In Latin, this was called *pollice verso*, which is roughly translated as "turned thumb."

Often the emperor took the audience's opinion into account. Judith Testa writes, "If thousands of thumbs went up, the emperor would graciously spare the defeated man's life, but if the crowd was feeling mean and the signal was 'thumbs down,' the emperor would indicate that the victorious gladiator should finish off his rival."[29]

Honor or Dishonor in Death

Throughout the day, as fights ended, slaves walked around the arena, making sure that defeated gladiators lying on the arena floor were indeed dead. According to some accounts of the time, the slaves killed off any warriors who were still alive, probably with swords or spears. However, they were careful to save as much blood as possible—gladiator blood was considered valuable for its alleged healing powers, and it was said that a bride whose hair was ritually parted by a sword dipped in this blood would enjoy good fortune.

The body of a gladiator who had died honorably received corresponding treatment. His corpse was taken out through a special gate and given a private hero's burial. But the bodies of criminals or other low-class fighters were simply dumped into mass graves or thrown into the Tiber River. To class-conscious Romans, it would have been unthinkable to bury a brave warrior's body in the same place as that of an executed criminal.

A deceased gladiator's weapons and armor were never discarded. These items were expensive and highly prized—much too valuable to throw away. Swords, helmets, nets, tridents, and other arms were kept, repaired, and passed on to new gladiators.

As for the slaughtered animals, their bodies likely piled up so quickly that they soon rotted in Rome's hot weather. Some of the meat from these creatures probably was donated to the poor people of Rome, and the rest was simply dumped in a pit.

Those Who Survived

For gladiators who survived, the rewards were great. A victorious gladiator was rewarded with lavish prizes such as money, gold, and golden palm leaves that symbolized triumph. Slaves who had been forced to become gladiators received an even greater gift: freedom.

But these victors were in the minority. The number of gladiators who died in the Colosseum is unknown, but it may have numbered in the hundreds of thousands. According to historian Philip Matyszak, "At least 10 humans and more than twice that many animals have died for every single one of its 48,440 square feet."[30] It has also been estimated that most gladiators died between the ages of 20 and 30. Some had fought as many as 30 or 35 battles. (At the time, the average Roman male lived to about the age of 48.) However, the lifespans of gladiators varied considerably. Some were said to have survived 100 or more battles before retiring.

Estimates suggest that this would have been unusual, however. Average professional gladiators likely fought only two or three contests a year. This would have given them long periods in which to recover from injuries, and it also kept the audience from seeing the same warriors over and over. Those gladiators who lived to fight another day were the superstars of their time among the ordinary citizens of Rome—popular, wealthy, and famous. Writer Nick Constable notes, "Most gladiators had a short career, but the few that survived . . . emerged as national heroes."[31]

Famous gladiators were notorious for being especially popular with women. Evidence of this is a surviving piece of graffiti that boasts of a particular gladiator's success in "netting" women at night. Women could become passionate over a certain gladiator even if he were dead. Accounts of the time assert that some women were so obsessed with their favorite fighter that they wore hairpins, shaped like swords or spears, that had been dipped in the blood of their departed hero.

The Colosseum saw hundreds, perhaps thousands, of gladiatorial contests and other performances during the most active period of its history. These games provided the people of Rome with rousing entertainment and the city's leaders with a measure of political power. Gradually, however, gladiator contests and other bloody entertainments fell out of favor with the Romans. As a result of this, and as a result of physical damage caused by natural events, in the coming centuries the grand Colosseum would fall into disuse and disrepair.

CHAPTER FOUR

The Colosseum in Decline

Immediately after its opening in the year 80, the Colosseum became a major part of Roman life. Less than two decades later, however, its popularity began a slow decline, and for many centuries afterward the stadium was ignored and unused. This slide into relative oblivion began with the end of the rule of Domitian in 96. Under the emperors who succeeded him, the Colosseum was used less and less for the kinds of lavish spectacle for which it was famous.

There were several reasons for this. For one, the cost of mounting ever more extravagant performances in the stadium was spiraling out of control. In particular, the cost of importing animals from Africa and the Middle East to Rome, always high, had become exorbitant. And the need to curb the spending on gladiator games was especially urgent in light of the enormous expenses that Rome's military actions were requiring. Rome was fighting a number of desperate wars to defend its far-flung empire from attacks by barbarian tribes, notably in portions of the Middle East and what is now Germany.

The Games Hang On

The Colosseum's drain on the imperial treasury did not end quickly, however. One early attempt to curb it came from Emperor Marcus

Aurelius, who ruled from 161 to 180. His desire to curtail expenses for gladiatorial combat was bolstered by his personal dislike for it. It is said that he found such games boring, a waste of time, and morally inexcusable. Because of this dislike, the emperor passed legislation in 177 that fixed prices for the sale of gladiators, making it more difficult to put on shows. Even though this new legislation meant a drop in the empire's income, Marcus Aurelius argued that Rome's treasury "should not be stained with the splashing of human blood" and that it was offensive to profit from what was "forbidden by all laws of gods and humans."[32] But Marcus Aurelius' attempt to cleanse Rome of its taste for bloodthirsty sport was unsuccessful, in large part because his son Commodus, who succeeded him, was eager to see the games continue.

By all accounts, Commodus had a sadistic streak that led to this love of grisly combat. He especially liked to make personal appearances in the arena, posing as a gladiator or hunter even though gladiators were considered among the lower classes. He fought rigged battles that ensured his victory, killing perhaps hundreds of animals and men. Reportedly, he paid himself so well for these appearances that a new tax had to be levied on his people. Chris Scarre notes of one such performance, "What should have been an entertainment (albeit of a grisly kind) was coupled with menace, as when he walked up to the seated senators brandishing a severed ostrich head in his left hand and a bloody sword in his right; meaning that he could kill senators, too, just as he had the ostrich."[33]

The games continued for some years even after the death of bloodthirsty Commodus, but succeeding emperors were forced to confront the empire's increasingly desperate need for money. The situation reached a turning point in the third century, when Rome experienced a period of serious crisis brought on by several factors: persistent threats from outside the empire's borders, civil war, famines, and a devastating epidemic of plague. The result was near chaos that nearly drained the treasury completely. Although the games were still popular with citizens, they were now simply unaffordable.

The Roman emperor Commodus (top left) fires an arrow to subdue a leopard during a well-attended show. Commodus liked to make personal appearances in the arena, often posing as a hunter or gladiator.

Enter Christianity

Another factor in the decline of the Colosseum's use as a showcase for gladiatorial combat also began to take shape in the third century. This was the increasing spread throughout the empire of a relatively new religion: Christianity. In the eyes of the church, the brutal gladiatorial games were wicked atrocities that ran counter to Christian beliefs. Church leaders, including Tertullian and Saint Augustine, asserted that the games were morally harmful and resembled pagan human sacrifice.

The decisive events in this aspect of the stadium's fortunes came early in the fourth century. One was the conversion of Emperor Constantine I to Christianity. Inspired by his newfound religion, Constantine made some unsuccessful efforts to ban gladiatorial combat. Historian David Potter comments, "Amongst the reforms of Constantine that are commonly regarded as 'anti-pagan' is an attempted ban on gladiatorial combat. The stress here must be upon the word 'attempted' since it has long been recognized that this ban was not effective. . . . Constantine's measure can be seen, at best, as a premature attempt to eliminate an activity that Christians found deeply distasteful."[34]

Despite this, evidence suggests that the most critical factor in Constantine's actions was actually economic, not religious. There are indications that Constantine was eager to use prisoners of war as slaves in his mines, rather than as gladiators. Judith Testa writes, "The Christians merely gave him [Constantine] an excuse to do something he wanted to do anyway. It was the collapsing economy of the empire, and not Christian conscience, that finally put an end to Roman blood sports."[35]

The Games Finally End

Despite Constantine's failure to ban gladiatorial games, the influence of Christian beliefs on the contests' future increased. A milestone came in the 390s when Emperor Theodosius I made Christianity the official religion of the empire. More and more, the deadly contests came under attack.

According to tradition, another major event occurred in the year 404. That year a Christian monk named Telemachus reportedly tried to stop a gladiatorial contest in the Colosseum by leaping into the arena and pulling the contestants apart, for which outrage the crowd stoned him to death. The emperor at the time, Honorius, was a Christian who was so moved by this incident that he completely banned gladiatorial battles, and that year saw the last recorded game.

The ban did not mean that all violent performances in the Colosseum came to an end, however. Staged fights and hunts, pitting animals against each other or against humans, continued to take place. According to some sources, though, wild creatures became so scarce toward the end of this period that common farm animals such as goats and pigs took the place of exotic African creatures. In 523 these staged battles and hunts also were banned.

After this ban took effect, editors had to settle for organizing relatively benign programs such as theatrical shows and chariot races. Fewer and fewer of these shows took place, however, and the

When Emperor Constantine I (pictured) converted to Christianity he tried to ban gladiatorial combat. The ban failed, but historians believe he, nevertheless, hastened the Colosseum's decline when he ordered slaves to work in his mines rather than train as gladiators.

Colosseum gradually fell into disuse. As it did, Rome's inclination to keep the stadium in good physical repair also declined, and it began to decay.

The Colosseum and the Empire in Decline

A series of natural disasters did much to speed this process of deterioration. One early catastrophe had already occurred in 217. That year the Colosseum was the scene of a major fire, possibly caused by lightning. Fiery timbers from the wooden upper story fell into the arena and burned so hotly that Rome's fire brigades, even though aided by sailors from the fleet at the nearby port of Misena, were unable to extinguish them before the structure's walls were badly damaged.

The destruction was so thorough that the Colosseum was unusable for the next six years. While repairs were under way, two other structures were used for games: a small stadium normally used for athletic contests and the Circus Maximus, usually the site of chariot races.

After the Colosseum was reopened in 223, partial repair work continued sporadically into the sixth century, but the stadium's overall condition continued to decline. Meanwhile, Roman stadiums throughout the empire suffered similar neglect, as the mighty realm itself slid into a dramatic decline and collapsed in the mid-400s.

As the empire as a whole collapsed, the once great city of Rome lost its own lofty position as the center of a mighty realm and a widespread religion. At its height, Rome had an estimated population of somewhere between 1 million and 2 million. But as the empire collapsed, hundreds of thousands of the city's residents died—victims of disease or starvation—or moved away in search of something better. By 400, Rome's population had dropped to eight hundred thousand, and by the middle of the 500s a mere thirty thousand people were left in the city.

The powerful political and religious leaders that once held sway over Rome—the emperor and the pope—were now antagonistic toward each other, squabbling often and ineffective at governing the city. And what had been one of the world's great cities was now little

"LIKE A SOFTENED SORROW"

During the nineteenth century many travelers considered the ruins of the Colosseum to be the most romantic sight in Rome. Many writers traveled to the Colosseum to experience its sad beauty. Among them was the British novelist Charles Dickens, who notes:

> It is no fiction, but plain, sober, honest Truth, to say: so suggestive and distinct is [the Colosseum] . . . as no language can describe. Its solitude, its awful beauty, and its utter desolation, strike upon the stranger the next moment, like a softened sorrow. . . .

> To see it crumbling there, an inch a year . . . is to see the ghost of old Rome, wicked wonderful old city, haunting the very ground on which its people trod. . . . Never, in its bloodiest prime, can the sight of the gigantic Colosseum, full and running over with the lustiest life, have moved one heart, as it must move all who look upon it now, a ruin. . . .

> As it tops the other ruins: standing there, a mountain among graves: so do its ancient influences outlive all other remnants of the old mythology and old butchery of Rome, in the nature of the fierce and cruel Roman people.

TheColosseum.net, "Famous Authors' Reflections on the Colosseum." www.the-colosseum.net.

more than a modest backwater. During this period, beset by barbarian invaders, many of Rome's most famous structures were destroyed, seriously damaged, or robbed of their valuable building materials. Only a handful of buildings remained to remind the Romans of their city's past glory, and the city would not significantly recover for centuries.

Multiple Uses

The Colosseum was perhaps the most prominent among the damaged and looted buildings of Rome. A series of major earthquakes in 847, 1231, and 1349 caused still more serious damage. The last of these quakes was especially devastating: It caused the outer wall on the south side to completely collapse. Elsewhere in the walls large cracks developed, and plants took root between the ruined travertine blocks. As before, limited repairs of the building were periodically attempted but never completed.

The Colosseum was by now completely abandoned as a location for spectacles. Instead it was used for a variety of mundane purposes. For a time the arcades under the seating housed a collection of small businesses, including shops and factories for cobblers and glue makers. Records indicate that parts of these areas were still being rented out as late as the twelfth century. At some point the stadium's arena was converted into a cemetery. Small houses also nestled inside the walls at various times. And the hypogeum, open now because the wooden floor of the arena had long since rotted away, was sometimes used for vegetable gardens or hay storage. This underground portion of the stadium in time became a dumping ground for animal dung and other refuse—so much so that over time it was completely buried.

In the early thirteenth century the entire building served another purpose. It was fortified and occupied as a castle by the Frangipani, a prosperous and politically powerful family. However, Pope Innocent IV took control of the building in the mid-thirteenth century, planning to use part of the site to build a hospital. But he was unable to fulfill this goal before his death, and the plan was abandoned.

Looting Building Materials

During its long period of decay, the Colosseum was generally not used as a stadium in any way, but there were a few exceptions. Notably, in 1332 a bullfight was held there to celebrate the visit of King Louis of Bavaria (in what is now Germany). According to an account of the time, eleven bulls and eighteen bullfighters died that day. In the mid-1600s a prominent church official hoped to stage more bullfights in the stadium, but a public outcry stopped that plan.

One unusual use for the Colosseum was proposed in the late sixteenth century. Allegedly to employ former prostitutes, Pope Sixtus V tried to transform the building into a cloth-making factory with workshops on the arena floor and living quarters in the upper stories. (Conflicting sources say that the cloth was to be either silk or wool.) However, the project was generally unpopular, and it was abandoned after the pope's death in 1590.

All the while, the stadium was being plundered for its valuable building materials. For example, the huge pockmarks in the building's exterior, which are still visible today, were created when the metal clamps that held the stonework together were hacked out of the walls by an invading barbarian tribe in 526. After that, Roman citizens felt free to reuse the lead and iron from the huge bolts remaining in the walls, as well as to recycle the stonework itself. Fik Meijer comments, "Anyone looking for building materials knew he had a good chance of finding something suitable at . . . the Colosseum."[36]

Sometimes it was the highest officials in Roman government and religion, not just ordinary people, who were the most eager to reuse the Colosseum's building materials. For example, some of the Colosseum—especially the elegant marble facade—was used to build new palaces, churches, hospitals, and other structures. Among these were such prominent buildings as the Cathedral of St. John Lateran, St. Peter's Basilica, the Palazzo Venezia (or Venetian Palace, which was used at the time as a residence for cardinals of the church), and military defenses along the Tiber River. According to records kept by Pope Nicholas V, between September 1451 and May 1452 alone a total of 2,522 tons (2,288 metric tons) of marble and stone were removed from the Colosseum and carted away.

Religious Significance

Despite these long centuries of decline and dismantlement, the significance of the Colosseum to Christians was never completely lost. Stories spread of Christian martyrs meeting their deaths at the hands of non-Christian Romans in the Colosseum. These martyrs, the stories said, had chosen to die rather than renounce their religious beliefs.

Although such stories have never been definitively proved, the site has long had important meaning for Christians for other reasons. By the late sixth century, for example, a small church had been built inside it. Another example involves Saint Gregory the Great, who was pope from 590 to 604. He is known to have sent holy relics from the stadium to a Christian emperor overseas, including a bag of sand from the arena that was supposed to bear traces of the blood of Christian martyrs.

However, later in the Middle Ages Christians apparently did not consider the stadium to be of special significance. Although a major religious route took Christian pilgrims to the Holy Land past the Colosseum, the building itself was not considered an important stop. In fact, many people during the Middle Ages believed a theory that the stadium was an ancient Roman temple to the sun god. This indifferent attitude changed in 1749, when Pope Benedict XIV announced that the Colosseum was indeed an important and sacred site because of its history as a site of martyrdom. Benedict ordered the construction of the Stations of the Cross, along with a large Christian cross, in the stadium.

After the pope sanctified the stadium, the looting of its materials essentially stopped. This was an ironic turn of events, since over the centuries a succession of popes had been responsible for looting the Colosseum for materials to build new churches and palaces. Archaeologist Keith Hopkins comments, "Indeed, it was the amphitheatre's reputation as a sacred spot where Christian martyrs had met their fate that saved the Colosseum from further depredations by Roman

Rome's famed Colosseum fell into disrepair with the collapse of the empire. One wall fell; elsewhere plants grew in cracks that formed between the bricks.

popes and aristocrats—anxious to use its once glistening stone for their palaces and churches."[37]

The Romance of the Colosseum

In addition to any religious significance, Rome—and the Italian Peninsula in general—had long had a romantic and artistic appeal to Europeans from outside the region. They loved its weather, its food, its relaxed atmosphere—and the remnants of its ancient architecture, especially the Colosseum. Testa comments, "Medieval pilgrims to the battered remains of the Eternal City [Rome] wrote of the Colosseum with awestruck admiration. Renaissance architects copied its architectural elements even as they stole its stonework. Painters sketched it and innumerable poets, Lord Byron among them, rhapsodized over it."[38]

During the nineteenth century this infatuation with the Colosseum and Italy in general grew even stronger among both Europeans and Americans. They romanticized the famous ruined stadium, and most who wrote about it agreed that it was best viewed in moonlight. Tourists flocked there to absorb its romantic atmosphere. Writer John Pearson comments, "It was the perfect tourist spot, the most sublime romantic ruin in the world. . . . Picturesque beggars, overgrown decay, even a broken pillar on which to sit . . . it was too good to last."[39]

WORDS IN CONTEXT

sanctified
Declared sacred.

Other notable writers of the era, including Charles Dickens and Mark Twain, were full of high praise for the Colosseum as well. Dickens was especially passionate, declaring, "It is the most impressive, the most stately, the most solemn, grand, majestic, mournful sight conceivable."[40]

In large part because of this infatuation with the stadium's beauty and importance in history, interest in restoring and preserving the Colosseum was strong throughout the nineteenth century. This interest was especially keen among archaeologists and historians from England, France, and Italy. For example, when the armies of French emperor Napoleon I occupied Italy in the early 1800s, he ordered archaeological work done at the Colosseum to explore its history and restore it physically. He dreamed of making the stadium part of a massive archaeological park. Beginning in 1805 Napoleon succeeded in completing some work, including the removal of the large cross, a small religious shrine, and the Stations of the Cross, until the authority of the pope was reinstated over the Colosseum in 1814.

In the mid-1800s Pope Gregory XVI ordered more significant work done. This included filling in the brick and marble of the building's walls, making them once again continuous all the way around. Previously, anyone could wander freely in and out of a huge hole on the south side of the stadium.

However, not all of the projects undertaken during the nineteenth century were successful. Notably, archaeologists were unable to reach the hypogeum. Its existence was known, but its function was poorly understood and it lay buried under some 40 feet (12.2 m) of earth and ancient trash. In 1813 and 1874 attempts were made to dig it out, but these were unsuccessful because the ground kept flooding.

The Plants of the Colosseum

One unusual aspect of the restoration work during this period involved bringing order to a surprisingly wide range of flora that had taken root in the building's nooks and crannies. Many of these plants were exotic species not normally found in Italy. The reasons for their appearance in the Colosseum's walls and floor are unclear. One theory postulates that seeds from African plants were carried to Rome in the fur, food, and cages of animals destined for the arena.

 STARTING TO END THE BLOODSHED

In AD 325 Emperor Constantine I tried to end the bloody practice of gladiatorial games. His recent conversion to Christianity, which considered such bloodthirsty games immoral, was one of the main reasons behind this. But Constantine was also eager to use prisoners of war as laborers in his mines rather than sacrifice them on the playing field in gladiatorial entertainment. Constantine's edict stated, in part, "At a time when peace reigns everywhere and internal order has been restored, bloody shows cannot delight us. Therefore we totally forbid the existence of gladiators; see to it that persons who up until now were condemned to live as gladiators for their crimes are sent to the mines, so that they can pay for their criminal behaviour without their blood being spilt."

Even after this pronouncement, the contests did not end immediately. Public interest in them was waning, but they remained popular enough to warrant continuance. The last recorded gladiator game was in 404.

Fik Meijer, *Gladiators: History's Most Deadly Sport*. New York: Thomas Dunne, 2003, p. 202.

No matter how they came to be in the Colosseum, hundreds of different kinds of flowers and other plants flourished there. In 1855 a British botanist, Richard Deakin, claimed to have identified and documented over 420 species in his book *Flora of the Colosseum*. Not surprisingly, the nineteenth-century visitors who enthused over the Colosseum's romantic airs considered these plants part of the structure's charm. Dickens writes of "its walls and arches overgrown with green . . . the long grass growing in its porches; young trees of yesterday, springing up on its ragged parapets, and bearing fruit."[41]

Despite Dickens's fondness for this vegetation, it is fortunate for preservationists that the bulk of it was removed or tidied. Otherwise, plants would likely have taken over to the point where the Colosseum could have been completely covered by them.

Another example of a nineteenth-century restoration project was a successful operation in 1807 to reinforce the building's facade with triangular brick wedges. And another uncovered a pit into which slaughtered animals, criminals, and slaves had been tossed in the days of the gladiators. Although many centuries had passed since the corpses had been deposited there, they still proved to be a powerful presence. Norma Goldman comments, "When the site was excavated . . . the excavators could only work a few hours at a time, for the stench was still so strong."[42]

This and other restoration projects of the nineteenth century were attempts to rectify the Colosseum's centuries-long physical decline, a decline that had occurred alongside its decline as an important historical monument. Happily for the modern world, restoration work on the magnificent building continued into the twentieth century and has continued up to the present day.

CHAPTER FIVE

The Colosseum Today

As the nineteenth-century enthusiasm for restoring the Colosseum continued into the early part of the twentieth century, the most significant work was done in the 1920s and 1930s under the direction of Benito Mussolini. Mussolini was the dictator of Italy before and during World War II, heading the dominant political party, the Fascists.

Mussolini was fanatically interested in reviving what he saw as Italy's vanished patriotism. The dictator idolized the emperors of ancient Rome and saw the restoration of the Colosseum as a way to bring back the glory of that era. He stated, "It is not rhetoric to say that the spirit of the new Italy is reconnected to that of ancient Rome, whose stones acquire once again the life and valor of twenty centuries ago."[43]

Mussolini's Project

The results of Mussolini's efforts to restore the Colosseum were mixed. One positive outcome is that the archaeologists under his direction cleared the hypogeum of its thick covering of earth and trash, exposing its underground chambers for future research and restoration.

But Mussolini's grand vision also had disastrous unforeseen consequences. In part because he wanted to link the Colosseum both physically and symbolically with his headquarters in the Palazzo

Venetia (Venetian Palace), the dictator ordered the destruction of much of the surrounding district and the construction of a major new road, now called Via dei Fori Imperiali (Road of the Imperial Forum), between the two. As a result, the stadium has suffered significant environmental damage due to the road's proximity. Judith Testa comments, "This [the road] exposed the stonework to hazards almost as harmful as the barbarians of earlier centuries: vibrations and automobile pollution."[44]

Unraveling the Colosseum's Secrets

During World War II the Colosseum was used variously as a bomb shelter and as a weapons storage facility, but after the war it once again became the subject of restoration, archaeological digs, and research projects. As archaeologists have worked in the area around the Colosseum—and, indeed, all over Rome—they continue to uncover many priceless artifacts, including the skeletons of fallen gladiators and animals. Mosaics, pottery, and other precious objects have also been unearthed over the years. For example, in 2011 a huge mosaic-covered wall was found near the Colosseum, depicting the Greek god Apollo, among other figures. The part that has so far been uncovered is 53 feet (16 m) wide and at least 6.6 feet (2 m) high. Researchers think that it may continue down as much as 26.5 feet (8 m) more.

Restoration work begun in 2012 of a passageway in the Colosseum has revealed even more treasures. These include traces of red, black, green, and blue paintings on the walls—as well as graffiti. The earliest of these that has been definitely dated is from 1620, although there are traces of others that may be from the third century AD. As a result of these findings, some archaeologists have speculated that the inside passageways where spectators walked to get to their seats were once even more colorful than previously believed.

Italian dictator Benito Mussolini (center) rides at the head of his troops in a 1932 parade near the Colosseum. Mussolini believed that restoration of the once-great structure would bring back the glory of ancient Rome.

The ancient paintings had been covered by centuries' worth of grime and moss growth, which had made the passageway appear to be a uniform greyish green. Although they are not as beautiful as the mosaic of Apollo and other artifacts uncovered near the Colosseum, discoveries such as this one prove that even a monument as familiar and carefully studied as the Colosseum can still hold secrets and surprises.

Solving a Riddle

In addition to this active archaeological fieldwork, a number of research projects are also being carried out. They aim to unravel the many mysteries the stadium holds. Through these studies archaeologists hope to answer tantalizing questions about how the Colosseum operated. One such project is seeking to understand exactly how the Colosseum's retractable awning might have worked.

Two theories about this were tested in the 1990s in two places: a fifteenth-century bullring in Barcarrota, Spain, and a well-preserved Roman stadium in Nimes, France. In one part of the experiment, cloth was attached to horizontal masts around the perimeter of the ring and furled out over the seats like a ship's sails. In the other experiment, the masts supported a "spider's web" of miles of ropes on which the sails were hung. In both cases, researchers used rigging that was based entirely on existing drawings from the Roman period. All of this rigging would have been familiar to a sailor from that era. The experimenters concluded that the horizontal mast setup was almost certainly the one used, not the "spider's web" model. They came to this conclusion in part because of the existence of holes in the upper parts of the walls facing the arena, which almost certainly were for steadying the horizontal masts. Also, the "spider's web" theory is unlikely because the bollards outside the stadium that would have held ropes in place were not sunk deeply enough in the ground to have supported the enormous weight of the awning.

WORDS IN CONTEXT

rigging
An arrangement of ropes such as is used on sailing ships.

Modern Restoration

Along with research projects like this one, Italian authorities have continued to organize increasingly large restoration projects to repair damage to the stadium. One notable example of this was carried out between 1993 and 2000. The main goal was to offset deterioration caused by pollution, especially from automobile traffic. However, the project had only limited success, and many problems remain. For example, in addition to the damage caused by air pollution, the Colosseum is facing a challenge to its basic structural support. The building's foundation is slowly sinking on the south side, which is now about 16 inches (40.6 cm) lower than the north. There is speculation that a crack may exist in the base of the stadium. Professor Giorgio Monti, a specialist in structural engineering, told reporters, "The concrete foundation on which the Colosseum is built is an oval-shaped 'doughnut' which is 13 metres [42 feet] thick. There could be a

⬡ A ZONE OF RESPECT

Rome's authorities have long authorized projects designed to restore and protect the physical Colosseum. But many observers have pointed out that another, less tangible aspect to the stadium's preservation deserves consideration: the threat to its dignity. Archaeologist Alberto Prieto comments,

> The Colosseum's imminent makeover has caused a lot of collateral [accompanying] controversy: there is increasing awareness of not only the monument's precarious condition, but also its image around the world. In the spring, [Rome's] authorities created a "zone of respect" around the Colosseum where the quaintly dressed "gladiators" and "centurions" who pose for photographs with tourists can no longer ply their trade. The city is also under pressure to remove the numerous trinket stands and mobile snack bars that dot the entire length of Via dei Fori Imperiali.

Alberto Prieto, "Sanguis et Harena: Fighting Around (and Over) the Colosseum," American Institute for Roman Culture, August 2012. http://saverome.wordpress.com.

stress fracture inside it."[45] This problem is aggravated by the continuing effects of vibrations from heavy traffic and a nearby subway line. One proposed solution is to establish a pedestrian-only zone around the Colosseum and the plaza surrounding it.

In the meantime, several smaller steps toward preservation and safety have been taken. For example, small bits of stone and plaster sometimes fall from the outside of the wall, especially if rain or snow seeps into the stone and makes it porous. So experts authorized a metal barrier to ring the monument at varying distances of 6 to 15 yards (5.5 to 13.7 m) from the outer wall. Although this will prevent visitors from touching the ancient wall, it will also protect them from falling debris. Mariarosaria Barbera, an Italian cultural heritage official, notes, "Where the Colosseum is highest, the distance will be greater—a fragment that falls from 50 metres has a different trajectory to one that falls from a height of 15 metres."[46]

The Biggest Restoration Project to Date

Measures such as this metal ring, however, are dwarfed by a plan, announced in 2011, that will be the most ambitious restoration project yet for the Colosseum. Carried out in several phases so that the structure can remain open to visitors throughout, it will be a dramatic change. For one thing, workers will remove decades of grime from the stadium's massive stone walls. This will restore its outward appearance as closely as possible to what the original wall looked like: a brilliant white. The project will also put into place body scanners and other security measures. These are needed because of sharply increased numbers of tourists as well as dangers such as the bomb threat that shut down the monument for two hours in 2011.

But the most important part of the project will open up parts of the stadium that the public has never seen. In 2011 small portions of the hypogeum and the top story were opened to the public for the first time. This was more than the public could previously access, but it was still only about 35 percent of the Colosseum—the rest was off-limits because of safety concerns.

However, by 2014, when the renovation project is scheduled to end, roughly 85 percent of the stadium's total area will be open to the public. In particular, visitors will be able to climb to the stadium's third tier, and small groups will be able to descend into the hypogeum. Writer Ann Natanson comments, "One of the world's great buildings will be revealed as never before."[47]

In a move that met with considerable skepticism, the Italian government announced that the project's main sponsor would be a commercial company: Tod's, a highly successful Italian luxury shoe company. The company pledged €25 million (approximately $US33 million in 2012 currency) toward the project's cost, with smaller amounts coming from other firms.

Many observers have been doubtful about the prospect of a private company spearheading a major project of this kind. Commercial firms have sometimes helped to underwrite high-profile restorations, but no project on this scale, anywhere in the world,

⬡ "WHICH BITS WERE BUILT WHEN"

Archaeologists and other researchers continue to plumb the secrets of the Colosseum, learning how, why, and when each part of its complex construction was completed. In some cases, it is clear what work was performed at a given point in time. Experts have documented at least a dozen different major building/reconstruction phases that took place over the centuries.

Often, however, it has been impossible to tell exactly what was uncovered or restored during a specific period. Archaeologists Keith Hopkins and Mary Beard comment, "The puzzle of dating the individual parts and the different phases has kept archaeologists amused for centuries. The truth is, though, that—despite the confident assertions of most guidebooks—it is now impossible to be certain which bits were built when."

Keith Hopkins and Mary Beard, *The Colosseum*. Cambridge, MA: Harvard University Press, 2005, p. 122.

In the modern age, pollution and vibrations from heavy traffic near the Colosseum have hastened the structure's deterioration. A restoration project in the 1990s sought to repair some of the damage. Another, more ambitious restoration effort is now under way.

had to date ever been paid for solely from private funding. Nonetheless, the strategy was widely considered necessary if the work was to be done. The Italian cultural ministry, which finances most preservation activities in the country, simply lacked the funds to complete the project.

When the plan was announced, many journalists and other observers wondered whether Italians would resent the fact that their government had employed a fashion house to pay for the upkeep of the Colosseum, perhaps the greatest of their cultural assets. But executives at Tod's promised that there would be no commercial considerations. Diego Della Valle, the company's president and CEO, told the *Wall Street Journal*,

You won't find a Tod's shoe or bag hanging from the Colosseum's walls. It's an undertaking with great cultural relevance and that's enough. We are ambassadors of Italy's life style and it's really our duty to give off a strong symbol. . . . People must stop reading about pieces of Italy's ancient ruins crumbling here and there. I like to think that Italy's other firms will follow the initiative. This country has a lot of beautiful things and we need to show that we can look after them.[48]

The Colosseum as a Tourist Attraction

Today, the Colosseum remains one of the world's most popular tourist attractions—so popular, in fact, that long lines to get in form from morning to evening. But the wait is apparently worth it: Some 6 million visitors pass through the Colosseum's entrance every year.

There is a small museum inside, and some informational kiosks. But of course the main attraction is the Colosseum itself. It is possible for visitors to simply walk around, but the experience is richer with guided tours, which are offered by an official tour company as well as other companies. Access to the newly opened hypogeum and the top story of the stadium is possible only with a guided tour, however, and these areas are not accessible for people with walking disabilities.

Coming to or leaving the Colosseum, tourists pass through a lively—as well as controversial—commercial scene. Vendors offer tourists all kinds of snacks as well as souvenirs, including keychains, illuminated plastic statues, and refrigerator magnets. Tour buses bring huge crowds of visitors in and whisk them away. And many local men stand around dressed as gladiators, offering to pose with tourists for photos. Although it is somewhat tacky, some view this commercial scene as a vast improvement over the bloody programs the arena once hosted. Writer Alan Epstein comments, "These days the show at the Colosseum mostly takes place, thank God, outside the structure."[49]

Recently, several ordinances have been passed in an effort to keep this outdoor commercial activity orderly. The "gladiators" who pose for photos must be licensed and can carry only plastic weapons. This is to stop the once-common practice of posing for photos for an agreed-upon price and then demanding additional payment afterward. These impersonators must also stay a certain distance away from the monument itself. And in 2012 a city law was passed that outlawed eating and drinking around monuments—including the Colosseum—that have historic, artistic, architectural, or cultural value. This is designed both to curb trash and to preserve a sense of dignity around these monuments. Antonio Gazzellone, a city council member, told reporters, "Rome needs to be protected, its beauty respected."[50]

Other Uses

Although the Colosseum is today mainly a tourist destination and a beloved symbol of the city, it is still on occasion in active use. For example, several concerts have been staged there in recent years. It is impossible to have shows inside the stadium for more than a tiny number of people. However, Elton John, Paul McCartney, Billy Joel, Ray Charles, and others have performed on stages set up outside the Colosseum, using its walls as a dramatic backdrop.

Also, many Christians continue to visit the Colosseum at least in part because of its religious connotations, despite a lack of definitive proof that any martyrdom ever occurred at the site. The pope continues to lead an annual torch-lit procession at the stadium on Good Friday, one of Christianity's holiest days.

The Colosseum on occasion also serves another purpose: It is a symbol of the international campaign against capital punishment. Italy no longer has a death penalty, and government authorities have authorized the use of the stadium to indicate their approval when another country rules against executing a prisoner. The color of the nighttime lighting around the Colosseum changes from white to gold whenever someone slated for execution, anywhere in the world, is released or is granted commutation.

And there is still another unusual use for the Colosseum today: It is a haven for hundreds of otherwise homeless cats. Cats are generally highly thought of in Italian society, and roughly two hundred of the creatures are in residence in the Colosseum's nooks and crannies at any given time, cared for by cat-loving Romans.

The Colosseum's brutal, glorious heyday lasted for only a few decades. But for most of its two-thousand-year history, the building's importance instead has rested in its power to remind the rest of the world of the magnificence of the mighty Roman Empire. Today, the Colosseum still serves this function: It is still the single most direct and dramatic link to one of the greatest, most fascinating periods in world history.

WORDS IN CONTEXT

commutation
Converting a criminal sentence; a death sentence that has been commuted removes the chance of execution.

SOURCE NOTES

Introduction: In the Days of the Gladiators

1. Judith Testa, *Rome Is Love Spelled Backward (Roma Amor)*. Dekalb: Northern Illinois University Press, 1998, p. 25.

Chapter One: The Roman Empire

2. Quoted in James Grout, "The Roman Gladiator," *Encyclopaedia Romana*. http://penelope.uchicago.edu.
3. Keith Hopkins and Mary Beard, *The Colosseum*. Cambridge, MA: Harvard University Press, 2005, p. 32.
4. Nigel Spivey, "Blood and Circuses," *Guardian (UK)*, March 11, 2005. www.guardian.co.uk.
5. Chris Scarre, *The Seventy Wonders of the Ancient World*. New York: Thames and Hudson,1999, p. 73.
6. Roman Colosseum, "Roman Colosseum History." http://roman colosseum.org.
7. Quoted in PBS, "Secrets of Lost Empires," *Nova*. www.pbs.org.
8. Quoted in Peter Connolly and Hazel Dodge, *The Ancient City: Life in Classical Athens & Rome*. Oxford: Oxford University Press, 1998, p. 190.
9. Fik Meijer, *Gladiators: History's Most Deadly Sport*. New York: Thomas Dunne, 2003, p. 16.
10. Quoted in Meijer, *Gladiators*, p. 14.
11. Quoted in Meijer, *Gladiators*, pp. 177–78.
12. Meijer, *Gladiators*, p. 39.
13. Quoted in Meijer, *Gladiators*, p. 40.
14. Quoted in Grout, "The Roman Gladiator."

Chapter Two: Design and Construction

15. Testa, *Rome Is Love Spelled Backward*, p.26.
16. Quoted in PBS, "Secrets of Lost Empires."

17. Scarre, *The Seventy Wonders of the Ancient World*, p. 170.
18. Connolly and Dodge, *The Ancient City*, p. 197.
19. Quoted in Tom Mueller, "Secrets of the Colosseum." *Smithsonian*. www.smithsonianmag.com.
20. Quoted in PBS, "Secrets of Lost Empires."

Chapter Three: The Spectacles

21. Quoted in Philip Matyszak, *Ancient Rome on Five Denarii a Day*. New York: Thames and Hudson, 2007, p. 81.
22. Hopkins and Beard, *The Colosseum*, p. 112.
23. Meijer, *Gladiators*, p. 138.
24. Quoted in Mueller, "Secrets of the Colosseum."
25. Mueller, "Secrets of the Colosseum."
26. Spivey, "Blood and Circuses."
27. Connolly and Dodge, "The Ancient City," p. 208.
28. Hopkins and Beard, *The Colosseum*, p. 76.
29. Testa, *Rome Is Love Spelled Backward*, p. 27.
30. Matyszak, *Ancient Rome on Five Denarii a Day*, p. 83.
31. Nick Constable, *Historical Atlas of Ancient Rome*. New York: Checkmark, 2003, p. 118.

Chapter Four: The Colosseum in Decline

32. Quoted in Hopkins and Beard, *The Colosseum*, p. 120.
33. Scarre, *The Seventy Wonders of the Ancient World*, p. 125.
34. David Potter, "Constantine and the Gladiators," *Classical Quarterly*, December 2010. www.academia.edu.
35. Testa, *Rome Is Love Spelled Backward*, p. 29.
36. Meijer, *Gladiators*, p. 209.
37. Keith Hopkins, "The Colosseum: Emblem of Rome." *BBC History*, www.bbc.co.uk/history/ancient/romans/colosseum_01.shtml.
38. Testa, *Rome Is Love Spelled Backward*, pp. 29–30.
39. John Pearson, *Arena: The Story of the Colosseum*, e-book. Bloomsbury Group. http://books.google.com.
40. Quoted in The-Colosseum.net, "Famous Authors' Reflections on the Colosseum." www.the-colosseum.net.

41. Quoted in TheColosseum.net, "Famous Authors' Reflections on the Colosseum."

42. Quoted in PBS, "Secrets of Lost Empires."

Chapter Five: The Colosseum Today

43. Quoted in Borden Painter, *Mussolini's Rome: Rebuilding the Eternal City*. New York: Palgrave Macmillan, 2007, p. 31.

44. Testa, *Rome Is Love Spelled Backward*, p. 30.

45. Quoted in Josephine McKenna, "Colosseum in Need of Urgent Support as One Side Is 15 Inches Lower than Other," *Telegraph* (UK), July 29, 2012. www.telegraph.co.uk.

46. Quoted in Nick Squires, "Colosseum Fence to Be Erected to Protect Tourists from Falling Masonry," *Telegraph* (UK), November 28, 2012. www.telegraph.co.uk.

47. Ann Natanson, "Restoring the Colosseum: A Colossal Undertaking," *History Today*, October 2011. www.historytoday.com.

48. Quoted in *Wall Street Journal*, "Tod's to Give Colosseum a Makeover," December 6, 2010. http://blogs.wsj.com.

49. Alan Epstein, *As the Romans Do*. New York: Morrow, 2000, p. 37.

50. Quoted in Elisabetta Povoledo, "Buon Appetito, but Not Next to the Monuments," *New York Times*, October 23, 2102. www.nytimes.com.

FACTS ABOUT THE ROMAN COLOSSEUM

Measurements
- Stadium is 615 feet (189 m) long, 510 feet (156 m) wide, and 164 feet (48 m) high.
- Arena is 272 feet (83 m) long and 157 feet (48 m) wide.
- Total area is 6 acres (2.4 ha).
- One Roman foot (called a *pes*) varied slightly by region, but it was generally around 11.5 inches (29.6 cm).

Weight
- Estimated weight of the common stone used in the walls is 750,000 tons (680,389 metric tons).
- Estimated weight of marble used in the walls is 8,000 tons (7,257 metric tons).
- Estimated weight of the concrete used in the walls is 6,000 tons (5,543 metric tons).
- Estimated total weight of the metal clamps used to set stones in the outer wall is 300 tons (272 metric tons).
- Estimated weight of cloth for the awning is 24 tons (21.7 metric tons).

Floor plans
- Estimated seating capacity: 50,000.
- Number of entrances: 80 (76 public).
- Number of above-ground floors: 4.
- Number of below-ground floors: 2.
- Average size of seat: 1.3 feet (40 cm) wide, 2.3 feet (70 cm) of leg-room.

Operations

- Number of trapdoors in arena: 36.
- Estimated number of sailors used to operate the awning: 1,000.
- Average number of bouts fought yearly by professional gladiators: 2–3.
- Number of yearly visitors today: more than 6 million.

FOR FURTHER RESEARCH

Books

Michael Burgan, *Life as a Gladiator: An Interactive History Adventure*. N. Mankato, MN: Capstone, 2010.

Will Mara, The *Romans: Technology of the Ancients*. Tarrytown, NY: Marshall Cavendish, 2011.

Marshall Cavendish Corporation, *Ancient Rome: An Illustrated History*. Tarrytown, NY: Marshall Cavendish, 2011.

Don Nardo, *Ancient Roman Art and Architecture*. Farmington Hills, MI: Lucent, 2012.

Don Nardo, *Roman Mythology*. Farmington Hills, MI: Lucent, 2012.

Liz Sonneborn, *The Romans*. Minneapolis: Lerner, 2010.

Websites

Colosseum: Deconstructed (www.history.com/videos/coliseum-de constructed). A series of short CGI-enhanced videos illustrating the building of the Colosseum.

The-colosseum.net (www.the-colosseum.net/idx-en.htm). An excellent series of essays, graphics, and articles curated by independent scholar Andrea Pepe.

Roman Colosseum, Greatbuildings.com (www.greatbuildings.com /buildings/Roman_Colosseum.html). This site has many excellent photos of the stadium.

A 360-Degree View of the Colosseum (http://microsite.smithso nianmag.com/content/Colosseum-Panorama/colosseum-1.html). This site, maintained by *Smithsonian* magazine, features 360-degree scrollable scenes inside and outside the Colosseum.

INDEX

PICTURE CREDITS

Cover: Thinkstock Images

Maury Aaseng: 37

akg-images/Newscom: 20

© Stefano Bianchetti/Corbis: 44, 73

© Christie's Images/Corbis: 52

© Stapleton Collection/Corbis: 59

Thinkstock Images: 6, 7, 10, 30, 78

Steve Zmina: 14

Nero (AD 37-68) holding a golden lute with Rome in flames, from 'Quo Vadis' by Henryk Sienkiewicz, published 1897 (oil on canvas), Pyle, Howard (1853-1911)/Delaware Art Museum, Wilmington, USA/ Gift of Mrs Richard C. DuPont/The Bridgeman Art Library: 16

Emperor Constantine I (c.274-337) the Great (mosaic), Byzantine/San Marco, Venice, Italy/Giraudon/The Bridgeman Art Library: 61

The Colosseum, Rome, Ducros, Abraham Louis Rudolph (1748-1810)/Private Collection/Photo © Agnew's, London, UK/The Bridgeman Art Library: 67

ABOUT THE AUTHOR

Adam Woog has written many books for children, young readers, and adults. He also teaches at a pre-school and writes a column about books for the *Seattle Times*. Woog and his wife, who have a grown daughter, live in Seattle, Washington.